WHAT ARE THE
Theologians
SAYING?

WHAT ARE THE

Theologians

SAYING

MONIKA HELLWIG

Pflaum/Standard, Dayton, Ohio

ISBN 0-8278-9051-6
90051/66M/S7.5M-7-173
Library of Congress Catalog Card Number: 78-114694
Pflaum/Standard Publishing, 38 West Fifth Street, Dayton, Ohio 45402

FOR
WINEFRIDE

Contents

Foreword

Christian theology walks a narrow ridge. It is concerned, in the first place, with a revelation of God claimed for Jewish circumstances, which was very shortly Gentilized in its interpretation as the price of its thrust beyond the Jewish community. It is carried on largely in intellectual categories, even though its primary business is the exposition of ideas contained in a faith which claims to be primarily a way to God—like its parent, Judaism, a mode of behavior and action—yet it does so by constructing a thought system which may at any point threaten the faith it serves. Mystical prayer, ecstatic behavior, and practical politics all have a place in Christian life. So, too, do cultural forms so disparate that one almost despairs of the possibility of a single faith tradition that can encompass them.

Yet Christian theology—a way of thought and discourse confined to one culture, the Greco-Roman with a slight Hebraic tinge—presumes to act as preserver, explorer, and guide to a faith intended, or so it keeps maintaining, for all men. If it succeeds it will do so hardly. It will also be marked by a proper modesty because of its realization that many theologies unborn are needed in the service of a faith that calls itself ''catholic.''

If the venture of theology is a risk, the venture of popularizing it is a greater one. For the theologian can count on a knowledge of history and philosophy among his peers, a received vocabulary of expression, and certain flexible limits of orthodoxy. The teacher of ordinary believers cannot presume on this equipment. Such a one must rely on the clarity of his or her thought processes and a mastery of ordinary, direct speech. There is a further hazard. In Christian circles a popular theology is already in possession in a way that the gospel of Jesus Christ is not. Put forward in creeds and catechisms and sermons, this theology is trustworthy in its origins and its intentions but often unfortunate in its effects. It normally leads to a brand of hyperorthodoxy which is in fact heterodox in certain particulars. This means that whoever presumes to transmit the work of theologians to ordinary people, provided the theologians concerned are not of the hyperorthodox and hence heterodox type, will encounter ready-made misunderstandings.

The gospel of Christ, whether in the version of the evangelists, Paul, or the other inspired writers, has a certain roominess about it. It can lead to heresy and has done so, as the history of the first five centuries has amply established. At the same time, the closing off of speculative avenues by doctrinal settlements has occasionally made it difficult to go back to the apostolic deliverance. As recent skirmishes over doctrinal handbooks have shown, the teachings of the New Testament unaccompanied by certain developments which they have resulted in over the centuries are not well received in every quarter.

The Catholic theologian does not read his Scriptures apart from post-biblical tradition because they are themselves the result of a process of tradition. Nonetheless, he is not committed to the vigor of every development that ever took place in an ecclesiastical framework, either within or outside of the New Testament period, any more than he feels it necessary to repudiate every tradition that has sprung up outside of Catholic church life. Yet some would have him confine himself in this fashion, a fact which does not make his life easier.

The theological writer's task is hard, but that of his interpreter to wider populations is impossible.

Dr. Hellwig has achieved her impossible task with a certain distinction. There is no traducing in her transmission, no treason in her translation. She reads her theologians with a clear eye and reports their views with a clarity of speech they might themselves envy. It is all done with ease and simplicity. It is never facile or simplified.

All this is because Dr. Hellwig is a theologian. Such is the requirement of anyone who would translate the works of theologians, either from another tongue or—much more difficult—as they appear in one's own tongue, into comprehensible terms. Because she is capable of independent theological work she hears other voices. If she could not initiate in this field she would be unable to pass the content of what she hears on to others.

It is a pleasure, then, to recommend to readers this helpful book on what the theologians are saying. The ones reported here are saying that Jesus Christ is Lord, a proposition which for an infinite variety of reasons cannot be expected to be popular in any age.

> Gerard S. Sloyan
> Professor of Religion
> Temple University

Introduction

This is a book for Catholic adults who want to understand the changing focus in Catholic theology, but who have no specialized training in theology. The book treats some of the basic questions theologians have been working on. These are not always the immediate practical questions, but the more fundamental ones that must be asked before the practical ones can be solved.

Only Catholic authors are discussed in this book, though it is true that some of the ideas originated with Protestants. Moreover, the authors chosen are not in all cases the greatest or most original scholars; the selection is biased in favor of the more lucid and readable, in the hope that some readers of this book will go on to read these authors for themselves.

This book is planned in ten short chapters, each more or less complete in itself. The plan is geared to parish adult education courses and discussion groups. You are strongly advised to read one chapter at a time, think it through and discuss it with others who have read it, before going on to the next chapter. A good way of conducting such a discussion is to divide the class or group into circles of no more than eight persons. Before engaging in discussion, go round the circle, giving each person a chance to state briefly what this chapter meant to him or her, and in what ways it does or does not fit in with his previous understanding of Catholic doctrine.

This kind of discussion will be profitable in any case, but it will be doubly so if the further discussion (after the initial response of each participant) can be guided by someone expert in contemporary theology.

ONE

Can the Church's Teachings Change?

JOHN HENRY NEWMAN, KARL RAHNER, BERNARD LONERGAN

Many good and intelligent Catholics are worried these days. We all know that secular society changes its laws, its structures, and some of its beliefs. But most of us had thought that the Church was quite different from secular society; that it did not change its laws, its structures, and its beliefs. We had come to expect that the answers given in the catechism would always be valid, because God guides the Church to teach the truth.

People worry when it seems that the Church's teachings are changing. They notice, for instance, a much more favorable attitude toward non-Catholics, a greater emphasis on the active role of the laity in Church matters, a relaxation of laws of fast and abstinence, official changes in the Mass, different explanations of traditional beliefs in sermons, and so on. In fact, people are entitled to worry about this. They are also entitled to ask many questions before accepting any such changes. Changes are not necessarily good. We need to know what we can change without losing the essentials. We need criteria that will tell us which changes are for the better and which are for the worse.

Theologians tell us that there is only one good way of

2 WHAT ARE THE THEOLOGIANS SAYING?

discovering these criteria or principles for judging changes to be good or bad. It is the common sense way of looking at the history of the Church's teachings. It is clear that these teachings developed very slowly and sometimes very stormily over the ages. Jesus did not give them to the Apostles in the shape of the creed or the catechism. The Apostles did not explain everything as it is explained now. Those who know enough of the history of ideas can even prove that the Apostles, and many generations after them, would not have understood the catechism at all. They might have said quite angrily that it contradicted the simple teachings of Jesus and made everything complicated to scandalize the ordinary followers of Jesus. They might even have banned the catechism as a dangerous heretical document.

Yet as we grew up, the catechism of the Council of Trent, adapted for us as the Baltimore Catechism, was accepted as the standard teaching of the Church on beliefs and on morals. It is quite clear that the teaching of the Church has constantly changed, and that we can expect it to continue to change. But if we want to understand what is happening now, it is crucially important to ask by what process the explanations of belief and the rules of morality changed in the past.

Even in the nineteenth century, Cardinal John Henry Newman was very much concerned about this. As an Anglican, wondering about the claims of the Roman Catholic Church to make pronouncements in doctrine, he asked himself constantly how one would know what was a true development of doctrine and what was a corruption or superstition that betrayed the Christian message. At that time Protestants, including some Anglicans, were accusing the Catholics of being the ones who kept changing the teachings of Jesus. In his *Essay on the Development of Christian Doctrine*, Newman laid down some principles by which one might judge whether a new formulation was a good development of an older doctrine or a corruption of it. His basic point of view was this: doctrines are ideas, and ideas always change because they exist, not in books, but in people. Moreover, the ideas change according to the way the people change, according to their different experiences and the new insights and understanding that follow from those experiences. When man's experience of living in the world changes because of new inventions and scientific discoveries, his ideas about everything will be shaped differently.

An example of this is man's understanding of divine providence. Before men understood what caused thunder and lightning and earthquakes, they were inclined to understand God's presence in their lives directly through nature, as though God were sitting in heaven responding to each human situation by throwing a thunderbolt, or flashing lightning, or turning on rain or sunshine. A person, or a whole society, who begins to understand the laws that govern atmospheric conditions does not have to surrender any faith in divine providence, but does have to express it and think about it quite differently.

A more old fashioned person in the same society might think everyone had become godless and atheistic because people no longer made the sign of the cross when they saw lightning, or said "God willing" when they spoke of plans for the future. Yet such a person would be making too sweeping a judgment. There might be truer understanding and greater faith than ever before.

Newman's criteria for judging what is a true development would be quite complicated to apply, but others have worked with his ideas since then. Moreover, in an essay written about fifteen years later, *On Consulting the Faithful in Matters of Doctrine*, Newman gave a very important insight from his own careful and scholarly knowledge of the history of ideas within Christianity. He pointed out that in the past, in the ages of the great heresies, the true faith always emerged again from deep down in the heart of the great community of the Christian faithful, who were not acquainted with the subtleties and technical language of theology at all.

In our own time, the great Austrian Jesuit theologian, Karl Rahner, has taken up the question again. He began with the position that we know now what it was in the past that led to the present official, orthodox teaching of the Church. Then he argued that whatever development was necessary in the past, in order to bring us to the present official position, is a lawful development and very likely to be necessary again. This way Rahner suggests we can work out some principles as to what is lawful and necessary change in the teachings in our time.

In his paper "The Development of Dogma," available in the first volume of his *Theological Investigations*, Rahner begins to work this out, though he certainly has not completed the task up to this time. He takes the development of doctrine that we can see within the New Testament as a model of what development of doctrine can and should be, because the New Testament is given to us to show us what Christian belief and life should be. The most important point that Rahner makes is that the development of the Church's teachings is more than simply logical. It always used to be said that the Church through the ages teaches the same doctrine but continues to make explicit what was already implicit.

One example would be Peter's statement in a sermon that God had raised Jesus from the dead. It is implicit in the words of the sermon that Jesus has really died, and the Creed makes Christ's death explicit with the words, "was crucified, died and was buried." In this example, the death is made explicit simply by logically thinking out what is already contained in the words spoken. But Rahner insists that there has been much development of doctrine in the Church that cannot be explained only by showing what was contained in the words of previous formulations.

What is handed down to us in the Christian tradition is much more than words; it is a whole way of life. The more we live it, the more we understand and try to formulate in words what is involved. Doctrine develops not only when people study the words already written in books, trying to reflect on their further implications. The most important way that doctrine develops is when people reflect on their life experiences.

An example that is not purely religious is that of love between man and woman, or between parent and child. This love has been described by psychologists, philosophers, poets. It is true that one might develop one's understanding and express further realizations about love by studying books. It is also true that the psychologist and the philosopher can explain the phenomenon with greater precision than most in their use of words. But we all know by common sense that the immediate and most realistic way to know about love is to experience that love. Moreover, we know by common sense that the psychologist and the philosopher would have no knowledge at all apart from the experience of those who have lived this kind of love in their own lives.

An example that is directly religious is that of prayer. The Church has developed quite an elaborate theology of prayer, but what we have learned through the ages that is new has been learned not so much because of the people who studied and argued about prayer but because of the people who prayed. It is also quite important to realize that the development in this case has seldom been smooth. Almost all our great mystics who gave expression to what they learned in prayer were denounced in their lifetimes as heretical and quite dangerous to the faith of simple people. They were denounced because the words they spoke sounded so new and different, and the experts on the theory of prayer knew that what the mystics were saying could not simply be deduced from the words of the official theology.

Newman, Rahner, and others have pointed out that from the time of the Apostles to the present, there have always been three parties involved in the development of doctrine: the whole community of the faithful, who were trying to live according to the gospel; the theologians, who were trying to make the theology more complete and clear; and the Church authorities, who intervened from time to time to select one explanation as the official one.

Perhaps the best insight as to how these three forces can and must work together has been given by Bernard Lonergan, a Canadian Jesuit philosopher and theologian. Few people have read much that has been written by him because a good deal of his works is available only in Latin, and what has been published in English is written, for the most part, in technical and difficult language. However, some of his ideas are not technical and difficult but simple and illuminating on all kinds of problems that people are worrying about.

In his Latin treatise on the Trinity, Lonergan suggests that Christian doctrine really develops in a kind of spiraling movement in three phases, which he calls transcultural, theological, and dogmatic. The fundamental level is the transcultural, which is the level of the ordinary human experience. Each generation is "catechized" or taught an explanation of the Christian faith and way of life. This explanation is in terms of our understanding, at that time, of the physical universe, of mankind and human potential, of society and personal relationships, of logic, of space and time, and so on. Again and again, as we learn new things about the world and about ourselves, we have to question and review our understanding of everything including our Christian faith. Again and again, sincere believers suddenly realize that there is something in the way their faith has been formulated that does not make sense to them in

terms of their experience of life. It is right and necessary
that they should say this; all through the ages they have,
in fact, said it; and it is this apparent problem that has
set the theologians to work to reconsider the way things
were expressed.

A very clear example is that of the theory of evolution
in modern times. The Bible is very dramatic in describing
"the beginning"; it speaks of God making things with his
hands, out of clay, and with his voice, out of darkness.
When theologians of an earlier age set out to give a clear
account of the doctrine of creation, they were already
aware that God does not have hands or a voice, so they
knew that this part of the account in Genesis was poetic,
and not intended to be taken literally. They knew they
were taking nothing away from the power of God or the
force of the message by stating the doctrine of creation in
terms of God "willing" things into existence, rather than
calling with his voice and molding with his hands. According to the ordinary knowledge of the universe that men
then had, it could not possibly have occurred to the theologians or the Church authorities that, when Genesis speaks
of God creating in six days, and when it gives an itemized
list of what was made on each day, this was also poetic
rather than literally intended. In modern times, increasing
knowledge of the universe, and especially the rapidly ac-
cumulating evidence for the unified and organic evolution
of the universe and the things in it, simply caused many
Catholics to say that the particular explanations in which
the doctrine of creation was taught to them no longer made
sense to them. The church found it necessary, not to deny
the doctrine, but to reformulate it quite thoroughly so
that contemporary believers could take it seriously again
as part of their way of life, and would not be obliged to
stow it away at the back of their minds as an irrelevant
piece of information. Today, people feel more comfortable
with an account of creation that has incorporated all we

know of evolution. Twenty years ago many Catholics were still quite worried about it. Fifty years ago almost all Catholics thought the theory of evolution was basically contradictory to Catholic faith. There has been a transcultural development here.

The second phase of doctrinal development is the theological. Every believer participates in some way in the transcultural phase, but not all believers are trained and competent enough to take part in the theological development. When the faithful persistently say that existing explanations do not make sense in their lives any more, it is the signal to the theologians, who are specialists in theology, that it is time to reconsider why the formulations were made that way in the first place, what was the important message, and what historical circumstances led to its being formulated in that way. When the theologians have studied enough to have some reliable answers to these questions, they attempt to reformulate the doctrines in a way that is faithful to the Christian message and the whole Catholic tradition, but which is also up to date because it makes sense to contemporary believers.

This is not an easy task. Many theologians usually try to do it in different ways, according to the thought and experience that "their" people share with them. The way theologians think things out in Holland or Germany often does not make much sense to clergy and faithful in Italy and Spain, because the lives of the latter countries are still largely shaped by an understanding of the universe and of human society which has long passed away in northern Europe and America. On the other hand, the Dutch and German theologians tend to be easily understood and appreciated by intelligent and educated Catholics in America, because their experience of the world, of society and of their own lives, is quite similar to that of our rapidly moving technological culture.

Lonergan's third phase of doctrinal development is

that of dogmatic development. Because the experience of different kinds of believers is so different, and because the theologians therefore tend to develop such different formulations, there are often clashes between schools of theology. More particularly, those whose experience and thinking is more old fashioned will often be badly upset and worried by new ways of explaining things. Sooner or later, they will be sufficiently anxious that they will ask the official teaching authority in the Church to intervene and give the official version. They may turn to the bishop of their diocese, or to a group of bishops, or to the Holy See in one or other of its offices, or even to a Council of the whole Church, if there happens to be one in session. In this case it is, as a matter of experience all through the ages, very difficult and delicate for the teaching authority to know what to do.

In a formulation of doctrine there are usually many *possible* ways of expressing the truth; there has never really been only one *correct* way of doing it. The teaching authority in the Church does not receive any special revelations by direct communication in so many words as to the better or more prudent way to express the teachings handed down since Apostolic times. Those responsible have to make their own prudent judgments, under the guidance of the Holy Spirit, based on the whole tradition of faith. Even when infallibility is invoked on behalf of a statement by the Holy See or by a Council, it does not mean that this statement was made on the basis of a new revelation. It means that it claims to be the authentic interpretation of what the faith of the people as a whole has always explicitly been, or has always implied.

Generally, statements of the teaching authority of the Church tend to be conservative, because that is their characteristic role in the triple development outlined above. However, this does not mean that there really has been no dogmatic development. Dogmatic development is always behind the transcultural and theological, but it is a gen-

uine and constant movement. It must take third place
because there cannot be a judgment on something until it
has been discussed (which is the role of the theologians),
and it cannot be discussed until human experience has led
men to raise the question (which is the role of all the
faithful).

This raises a very important issue. Some people feel guilty
when they find themselves thinking differently from the
existing official pronouncements of the Church. They feel
they are lacking in faith or loyalty when their own experience leads them to see something in the official teaching
as contradictory or irrelevant to their lives. Yet they
should respectfully and thoughtfully express this sense of
incongruity, because this is the way the development of
doctrine has always taken place and must continue to take
place.

Moreover, some people are shocked to find theologians
discussing issues in language quite different from, and apparently contradictory to, official pronouncements. This
would only be wrong if we could be sure that there could
be no further dogmatic development. In fact, we never
have that certainty. Some people think the theologians
should only discuss what the teaching authority of the
Church proposes for them to discuss. This can only be
based on ignorance of how the three phases of doctrinal
development function, because experience must come first,
then reflection and discussion, and, only after that, judgment.

This process is complicated by the fact that life goes on
and we cannot predict all the possible developments. There
is often quite a time lag between the first experience of a
new way among the faithful of looking at life and the public discussion by theologians of new ways of formulating
doctrine to meet the new experience. There is also a time
lag between the beginning of the theological discussions on
a particular formulation of doctrine and the official pro-

nouncement about it by the Church. This means that by the time of the pronouncement, the living experience of Christians may already be far ahead of its historical development. The pronouncement may refer to issues that came up far in the past. This does not mean there is no purpose in such pronouncements. They are important and central in the whole tradition and give us our sense of direction. They should be accepted with the greatest respect because of their importance in maintaining balance and direction. But it means that even when a pronouncement comes out, we can expect that life will have moved beyond that point, and that the theologians will be trying to follow life.

Catholics sometimes think that there has been development of doctrine in the past but that the work of development has been completed in all but a few minor points. They think this for two reasons. One is that they themselves, within their own lifetimes, have not noticed anything changing. The other is that things seem to be worked out so explicitly and in so much detail that many Catholics cannot imagine what is left to develop further. Before the Second Vatican Council, this way of thinking was common. Since that time, everyone who has taken the trouble to study the documents with some professional guidance is convinced that doctrinal development is still going on in very important matters and that almost any issue may be opened up again for further discussion, because new horizons and new perspectives keep opening up in our experience.

With reference to the past, we can judge what was a true development. But for the present and the future we must live with risk, not having access to any absolute certainty. This means we must remain open to truth, no matter from whom or from where it may come. In other words, we must live in faith and hope.

Something that Newman, Rahner, and Lonergan have all

made quite clear for us is that the life and growth of the
Church, which includes especially the development of her
teaching, cannot be without conflict. Sometimes this conflict may be sharp and painful. Yet it need not involve
bitterness or hostility against persons who think and experience differently. It need not involve condemnations,
excommunications, or schisms. Those who have most fur-
thered the development of doctrine in the Church in the
long run have usually been persons who acted discretely,
patiently, and generously, but who never feared the truth
of their own experience, insight, and scholarship.

TWO

What Did God Really Reveal?

RENE LATOURELLE, GABRIEL MORAN

After reading and discussing the previous chapter, some Catholics will think that the most important point has been evaded. They will say that the Church's teaching can change about some matters, but not about those truths that God has revealed. These are eternal truths that remain the same forever.

It may not be immediately evident how much of our thinking depends on the way we understand revelation. Many contemporary theologians have written about revelation because they do not think it is at all obvious what we mean by the word. In the past theologians discussed which particular truths God had revealed, and whether we knew revelation through scripture alone or also through the living tradition of the Church. Today's theologians are much more concerned with the question: what is revelation?

We have always realized that it is Himself that God reveals. He shows Himself more clearly than He was known before, shows something about Himself that was hidden or simply not noticed before. He shows Himself as savior, as powerful and merciful, as gracious and generous, as making life worthwhile and giving real meaning to our exis-

13

tence. Does God do this by speaking words, or by events?
If He speaks words, how does He speak them? What language does He use? To whom does He speak? If He does not
speak actual words, but reveals by events, what is the difference between reason and revelation? What is the importance of the words we have in our creeds and in our
catechisms?

The Catholic Church officially turned its attention to
these questions at the Second Vatican Council in the dogmatic constitution on revelation. This document refers us
to the Bible to understand what revelation is, and refers to
the Bible as modern scripture scholarship has learned to
interpret it. It does not claim that all of the Bible is revelation nor that all of revelation is in the Bible. It only
claims that the Bible offers us the classic instance from
which we can understand how and what God reveals.

The Bible usually records events that happened in the
history of God's special people, such as the deliverance from
the Egyptian slavery, the achievement of a common iden-
tity in the wandering in the desert, the entry into the
promised land, and so on. Sometimes it records the same
events several times in different ways. The purpose of the
telling is usually not to give an accurate chronicle of all the
events, but rather to give an interpretation of how clearly
God's mercy and faithfulness and love for His people
were made manifest in this happening. In the account of
the crossing of the sea of reeds in Exodus 14, for instance,
it is really never clear whether the people of Israel were
able to get through because an easterly wind cleared the
waterbed, or whether the waters parted instantaneously
when Moses stretched out his rod, or whether the people
saw the intervention of an angel. The narrator seems completely unconcerned about giving a factual account of the
crossing, perhaps because what was important to him was
that through their escape from slavery the people realized
God's care for them and for their destiny.

Professor René Latourelle of the Gregorian University in Rome, in his book *Theology of Revelation*, points out three very important aspects of the biblical understanding of revelation. First of all, it is quite clear that there is a progressive understanding of what revelation is all about; the God who reveals Himself becomes more and more personal in the kinds of demands that He makes. From the Christian perspective of the New Testament, these demands find their concrete and final definition in the person of Jesus, who speaks clear words in a human language and gives ordinary human signs of love and trust and challenge. If scripture gives classic texts to show the meaning of revelation, then we must conclude from this that it is the nature of revelation in all our lives to be progressive. It will consist of signs that become gradually clearer and of demands that become more specific and more far-reaching, for each of us and for all of us together.

Secondly Father Latourelle points out, scripture speaks mainly of God revealing Himself in the particular history of the people of God, but it keeps referring back to the word of God already spoken in creation. Not only Genesis, but also the Psalms and the other books of the Wisdom literature, make frequent reference to this revealing of God in the work of creation, and the New Testament writers keep echoing the Hebrew scriptures in this. What is clarified and brought to focus in the special events told in the Bible is continuous with the rest of experience and makes sense of the whole of human experience and human existence.

A third very important point emerges in Latourelle's discussion. The events of history do not, by themselves, constitute revelation; nor does the simple narration of these events constitute revelation. It is only by prophetic interpretation that they become revelatory. The prophet is one who speaks for God, telling the meaning of the events that are happening. This is why, for instance, Roman or Syrian records of the Maccabean wars would not be testimony of God's revelation to us, while the Jewish accounts do give such testimony.

This raises the further question as to how people come to speak for God, how they know what to say, and how particular words and expressions become canonical, or binding, for the whole tradition. This is really the main question concerning the process of revelation and how we are to understand it. It is precisely this question which is the topic of the book by Dr. Gabriel Moran of Manhattan College, which, like Latourelle's book, is entitled *Theology of Revelation.*

Brother Moran maintains that revelation is a constant dialog or conversation that is always going on between God and man, and that the center of that conversation is Jesus Christ. Jesus is in the world not simply to bring or pass along revelation like a message relayed from heaven; he is in the world to *be* revelation. He is a happening and he gives his own prophetic interpretation of himself. As a happening, he is a human being totally open to all the possibilities of being and love held out by God. As a prophetic interpretation, he explains the nature of God as a huge welcome to the existence and becoming of all men.

As a happening, Jesus is fully a man among men. Moran points out that this means that Jesus is, therefore, first and foremost the recipient of God's revelation. The Gospels show Jesus constantly praying to the Father, growing in wisdom, sometimes admitting that there were things he did not know, and gradually becoming more fully aware of his own mission and destiny. The whole New Testament shows Jesus living his life in such a way as to become constantly more fully aware of what all human existence is really about, and sharing that awareness with his followers and associates.

Our faith asserts that Jesus is Lord, uniquely Son of

God, and therefore the clear and definitive Word of God spoken in history. But this only makes sense if we understand that it is a fully human word that is spoken. Jesus struggled to express in Aramaic words, drawn from his culture and from his personal and social environment, his human understanding of the divine meaning of his own existence and life in the world. He also struggled to express that meaning in typical Jewish gestures and signs, and in the way he shaped his own life and responded to the way others shaped it.

When the Apostles pass on the message of Jesus in their sermons, they do not begin by reporting what he said. They first mention their own Easter experience, their participation in the Resurrection event. The revelation that they saw in Jesus was first and foremost his way of meeting death and his bursting the bonds of death. This is rather important; for them, the meaning of Jesus was something that could not be entirely contained in words. For them, revelation was something that could not be entirely communicated in words.

What was the revelation that the apostolic community actually received from Jesus? It was, first and foremost, the full human experience of his presence, his companionship, his friendship, lending meaning and purpose to their lives. Only secondarily, and within the context of this friendship, did they receive explanatory words in which Jesus gave his prophetic interpretation of the happening of his own presence in their midst.

How did the apostolic community receive the revelation of Jesus? First of all, by living in his company and living his way. Only by living his way did they come to reflect on his revelation and on the words he spoke; and because they reflected they gave utterance to the reality in their own words. Their own words were a further prophetic interpretation, extending the presence of Christ further into the world.

We have many of those words of the apostolic community, of course. We have a classic collection of them clearly defined in the New Testament. We also have a more elusive collection of the prophetic interpretations of the apostolic community which has been passed on to us by tradition. It consists of liturgical and catechetical formulas of all kinds (for instance, the creeds). As a testimony of the apostles, these formulas are more elusive because they have been elaborated and shaped and refined during the course of the centuries.

This raises a very important question about revelation. If a text or prayer or formula was elaborated after the time of the apostles, is it less sacred or "less revealed"? Did revelation stop when the apostles died and the next generation took over? Clearly, the interpretative words of the apostles are special, indeed unique, simply because of their personal presence at the center of the Christian event. If Jesus *is* the revelation of God because of the dialog or conversation of man with God that he achieved in his life as it unfolded, and because of the way that he met death and overcame it, then those who walked in his company had an experience that is definitive for all time. Christ radically changed our understanding of life in a way that it will not change again. The apostles are witnesses in a way no one else can be.

It is important, however, to realize that this testimony would have very little significance today, if it were only the account of a past event. What makes it significant is precisely the fact that we are participants in the same revelation that the apostles interpret to us. Their interpretations have meaning only to the extent that we share in the same happening and reflect on it and give our own prophetic interpretation, realizing the dialog of God and man here and now.

When the apostles passed on revelation, what was it they actually passed on? First and foremost, it was the happening. How does one pass on a happening? Their method was through the life of the community. They drew others in the group to share the way they lived, which was the way of Jesus, a life transformed by hope and purposefulness because of the resurrection experience. In the context of this sharing of life, they offered their interpretation in words, and the words they uttered took on meaning for those who joined them. Out of the living experience of that sharing of life in different times and different circumstances, each generation gave its own interpretation in words.

Clearly, in the course of time, those words of interpretation changed quite a lot. They changed according to the pattern sketched in the previous chapter. One might be tempted to ask at what point revelation ends and ordinary theology, liturgy, and catechetics begin. Yet this would really be a meaningless question similar to the question of where the woods end and the trees begin. The life of the Church, the constant struggle to live a life of love and trust, the celebration of life in this liturgy, and the explanation of it in theology and catechetics—all this *is* our participation in revelation. It is revelation itself.

This does not mean that revelation is simply a recording of what was revealed before; one which is played over again and again. Revelation is the living and intensely personal communion of men with God in which God communicates not some sort of factual information but the living reality of Himself. That sort of communication cannot be played over and over like an old recording.

Some people may have a further rather important question. If the whole participation in Christian life is part of revelation, then is every word and explanation just as good as any other? How do we know that people are not fooling themselves? And what becomes of the claims of the Catholic Church with its dogmatic teachings, its sacramental power, and its authoritative moral guidelines?

Although revelation is first of all a happening, it must be expressed in words, because all human understanding comes to focus in words. We cannot live a meaningful life without expressing it in words. Furthermore, words are always a community product and community property. My words have meaning because a society has agreed to a common meaning for them. When the Christian community wants to share its experience, it has to agree on the way it explains itself. It has to agree on its common understanding of the world, the community, its history and its future destiny, and most of all on its common understanding of God. The Christian community must have a common statement of its prophetic interpretation of the events in which God revealed Himself in the community—the events of the life of Jesus, of the original formation of the Church. It must also have a common prophetic interpretation of the ways in which God reveals Himself in the community to-day—through the sacraments and the life of charity of the Church.

Because the task of salvation is a community task, it serves no salvific purpose to create chaos and disrupt the unity of effort and understanding and life that have been achieved. In fact, our continued participation in the event of revelation is guaranteed precisely in the unity of the Church, and the unity of the Church requires continuity of teaching and authoritative judgments as to what is orthodox teaching and what is heterodox.

This position assumes that the continuity is guaranteed in a living dialog, and that authority unifies and harmonizes a vital personal involvement in the process of revelation. Continuity and unity would serve no purpose if they were an empty shell formed from past life now withered away in death. Revelation is real while it is alive, and it is alive while people are creatively participating in the encounter. But whenever people creatively participate, then new events happen, and new words are spoken and new visions are projected.

Revelation did not end when the apostles died out, simply because revelation is not a collection of factual information about situations beyond our experience, but the self-communication of the living God. Revelation was not cast into the unchanging pattern of a finished product, because it does not really consist of so many unchanging eternal truths but of the living reality of the one great eternal truth of God who is saving love.

Revelation was not exactly closed with the death of the last apostle but rather definitively opened, more or less as a love affair is not completed when two people marry but rather definitively begun.

THREE

How about Papal Infallibility?

YVES CONGAR, KARL RAHNER, HANS KÜNG

For the Catholic reader, the obvious question at this point is: how about papal infallibility? You may be well satisfied with the explanations, given in the first chapter, of how the Church's teachings change through the ages. You may also agree that what has been said in the second chapter, about what revelation is and the way it happens, makes sense. Yet you may have an uneasy feeling that a crucial point has somehow been evaded.

For many Catholics the explanations given in the first two chapters are acceptable as long as it is agreed that the process of revelation and the process of development of doctrine go just to a certain point and then quite abruptly stop. That certain point is the one at which the Pope speaks about a matter of doctrine, and the matter is closed. After that point is reached, many Catholics are convinced that no one should ever raise the matter again, not even an ecumenical council of the Church, or even another Pope.

Other Catholics believe that because situations change, what one Pope may have said in one situation in an earlier time may not really apply to the situation in which people are living now. Moreover, some Catholics are saying that culturally and socially, our present Pope is living in an earlier stage of history than the faithful of the northern European and North American world, and that he is teaching in the context of the world he knows. Thus, his teachings may not always be relevant to the rest of the world and to all people.

Besides this debate among Catholics, many Protestants are, once again, very much interested in the question of the papacy. At one time, most Protestants felt very strongly that there should be no such office as that of the Pope. Now times have changed. Many Protestants are very interested in the question of whether all churches need a world leader who is not just a functionary, like the president of the World Council of Churches, but is chosen as a holy man, a special person set aside as a spiritual figure, voicing the conscience of the Christian community about important questions in the world such as peace, hunger, and poverty.

Today, many people who are not Catholics listen with the greatest respect and hope to what the Pope has to say. They are glad to have him speak at the United Nations, and anxious to have him visit their countries and meet their civil and religious leaders, even in those lands whose people are mainly non-Christian.

But the non-Catholic peoples, especially Protestant Christians, are quite concerned over what they see of the Catholic attitude to infallibility. They constantly wonder whether we, as Catholics, are true to the revelation of Jesus Christ and the breath of the Holy Spirit in the Church in the way we regard the papal teachings.

For all these reasons, many contemporary Catholic theologians have devoted themselves to the question of papal infallibility. They have studied what exactly the First Vatican Council meant when it gave the formal definition of papal infallibility in the nineteenth century. They have also looked into the question of why this definition was made, and how it is related to the infallibility of the Councils of the Church and the infallibility of the faithful now and through the ages. Finally, and most important, theologians have studied very painstakingly the evidence that history gives us of the developing structure of the Church through the ages, and the ways in which the claim to the Roman primacy first arose, as well as what people seem to have meant by that claim at various times.

Karl Rahner, who was introduced in the first chapter of this book, has written a very important and readable little book, *The Christian of the Future.* In it he discusses the changing structure of the Church, and says that although official infallible pronouncements once served the purpose of the Church, they really do not serve this purpose any longer. He foresees that future Popes simply will not make such pronouncements and that the whole question of infallibility will cease to be an issue.

After the encyclical *Humanae Vitae* was issued, the German bishops asked the help of Karl Rahner. These bishops had issued a statement telling the people the importance of the encyclical and its purpose of protecting the sanctity of the person, the sanctity of marriage, and the sanctity and privacy of the home. In the statement they also pointed out to the people that the encyclical did not take away from them their ultimate personal decision of conscience in the matter of birth control. Some people had asked how this could be, when the Pope had given his judgment on the matter and the Pope is infallible. The bishops asked Karl Rahner to write articles in several German newspapers and explain the matter.

The explanation Rahner gave was really very simple and very traditional. He pointed out that the infallibility of the Pope, as recognized by Vatican I, applies only to solemn statements, usually called *ex cathedra,* in which the Pope explicitly claims that infallibility. Moreover, he can only claim it where it is clear that he is giving expression to the faith of the whole Church, that is, when he is speaking for the whole assembly of the faithful. As Rahner pointed out, Pope Paul did not claim infallibility in this statement, but simply gave his personal judgment. He could not have claimed infallibility because his commission, which had studied the tradition from the past and the evidence from the world community of the faithful in the present, had advised him to the contrary of his own judgment.

Some people, however, thought that even when the Pope did not explicitly claim infallibility, Catholics (including the theologians) should still consider his words infallible and stop all discussion at that point. Rahner's answer to this was that while Catholics should always listen to the teaching of the Pope with great respect, they would not be obeying Christ or the Church if they made no distinction between infallible and non-infallible teachings. They would be refusing to play their own role in the development of doctrine by leaving all the responsibility, unthinkingly, to one man.

This one man does not have the experience of married people and cannot even put their questions to the theologians unless some married people describe to him their experience and the questions that arise out of it. Neither does this one man have the expertise, time for research, or access to libraries and source materials that all the theologians have. If the entire Church waits for him to ask the right questions and find the right answers, many people are shirking their share of the responsibility and the risk. In that case they would really deserve to wait indefinitely for clear and helpful answers.

One source of confusion for many of us may be an incorrect way of understanding papal infallibility. An easy but entirely mistaken analogy is that the Pope has a private hot line to heaven, and when there is a special problem he presses the button, picks up the receiver, and gets a new

revelation which will solve the problem. When the Fathers
of Vatican I defined papal infallibility they knew that
the Pope's task was much more complicated than this,
and that the communication was not down from heaven,
but up from the tradition of the whole community of believers through the ages. They knew the Church had always taught that ''public revelation was closed with the
death of the last apostle,'' precisely in the sense that the
Church would not be given special answers from heaven
to new problems that would arise. Men would always have
to search the Scriptures and the tradition to find the answers.

As a matter of fact, theologians are generally agreed
that there have been only two papal statements that clearly
fall in the infallible category; the definition of the Immac-
ulate Conception in the nineteenth century and the definition of the Assumption of Mary into heaven in the
twentieth. In both these cases it is very clear that the
Popes claimed to be giving expression to the faith of the
whole Church as it could be traced back to apostolic times.
In neither case did they give a philosophical or theological explanation of exactly how these dogmas should be
interpreted. They gave voice to the faith of Catholic believers in exactly the images and symbolism that had been
used in statues, pictures, stained glass windows, and sermons.

In the images and symbolism concerning Mary, Catholics had found great inspiration because they realized that
what was being said about Mary expressed the ideals for
which the whole Christian community was striving. The
people who really prayed and meditated were not asking
whether Marian doctrines were to be interpreted in a
biological sense, because they knew that that had nothing
to do with the purpose for which the teachings were being
proposed to them. The papal definitions did not answer
those questions either, but simply encouraged the devotions

in which believers expressed their own striving to live in accord with the gospel.

A French Dominican, Father Yves Congar, in a book entitled *Tradition and the Traditions*, has helped to put the whole question of papal infallibility into historical perspective in our understanding of the Church. Father Congar first worked in the field of ecumenism before he became very much interested in the role of the laity in the Church. In his work he studied the structures of the Church and how they had taken on the shape they did. His study shows that there has always been a great deal more variety than most Catholics of our times (including the theologians and the canonists) had realized.

Because most Catholics had assumed a static and unified Church organization, it was also easy to assume that that pattern was more or less set by Christ and should never be changed. But when men study history and suddenly realize that it was all changing all the time, and that it looked very different indeed at some times, they have to ask further questions about what is the divine and necessary pattern of the Church, and what is simply a human attempt to organize life in a Christian community as best meets the need. Whatever falls in the latter category could, of course, be changed again and in the same way, when the needs of the times change.

This type of historical and theological study is still very much in progress among Catholic theologians. There are, for instance, many studies about the principle of collegiality and about the relation of the Pope to the whole college of bishops. Two of the most helpful and most careful studies that have been published recently are written by Hans Küng, and entitled *Structures of the Church* (published in English in 1964) and *The Church* (published in 1967). Father Küng is a Swiss theologian who has worked extensively in ecclesiology (the theology about the Church) and in ecumenism. In addition, he partici-

pated in the Second Vatican Council as adviser to his
bishop.

Hans Küng's studies, particularly the earlier one, help
to answer most people's questions about the teaching authority of the Church, in general; the Pope, in particular;
and the Pope when claiming to speak infallibly, in a very
special way. Küng points out that when Vatican I debated
and passed the constitution *Pater Aeternus*, there were
two issues at stake concerning the Pope. The first concerned
his power to command and rule in dioceses other than his
own diocese of Rome. Many problems remain concerning the
interpretation of Chapter III of the constitution, which
dealt with this question: concerning the Pope's relationships with the bishops, and concerning his relationships
with a council of the Church whenever one is in session,
whenever one has definitely legislated about something, or
whenever one has even laid down guiding principles. Chapter III, however, is not the issue most lay people are concerned with.

The second issue is the one that most lay Catholics want
to know more about, and which many lay Catholics are
anxious about. This is the issue of infallibility of teaching,
when the Pope solemnly and officially interprets Christian
doctrine. It is not possible to assume that the Pope cannot
make any mistakes or fall into heresy. The classic manual
on canon law by Wernz and Vidal gives this traditional
teaching within the Catholic Church: that if the Pope
falls into heresy, he must be deposed. Though the authors
think of deposition as a very unlikely thing to happen,
they are convinced that provision must be made for the
possibility. If they had held the ''hot line to heaven'' theory of papal infallibility, they could never have contem-
plated even the most remote possibility of a Pope falling
into heresy. Actually, as Father Küng demonstrates, many
Popes have been deposed in the past for various reasons.

The infallibility which the First Vatican Council rec-

ognized in the Pope is a severely limited one. This is especially interesting because some Catholics at that time,
including some bishops, had said that the Pope is always
infallible whenever he speaks, that he simply can never
make a mistake in teaching Christian doctrine. The Council clearly disagreed with this belief and attributed absolute infallibility only to God. It declared that the Pope
possesses that infallibility which God willed to give the
Church, whenever he solemnly and officially (*ex cathedra*)
defines a doctrine that must be held by the whole Church
concerning faith or morals.

The question concerning morals was considered harder
to pinpoint by the Fathers of the council than the one
concerning faith because it is rather difficult to determine
exactly what a doctrine concerning morals might be. But
the really important point to note about the definition is
that it recognizes that the Pope, when acting officially on
behalf of the whole Church, possesses that freedom from
error that the whole Church possesses. The Vatican Council
fathers did not think the Pope was above the Church, with
special access to truth, but that he could express the truth
that the Church already held. He could personally exercise
the teaching power, and did not have to assemble a
council before this power could be considered official.

The important question, then, is: what is the infallibility
of the Church to which the council made reference? The
Pope is, in fact, dependent on the faith of the whole
Church, from which he draws his understanding of revelation. The whole Church means just that. It means the people of God, the laity, with their bishops and priests and the
theologians, operating in the way already indicated in the
first chapter of this book.

From the previous chapters, it should be clear that some
further questions about infallibility are related to our
understanding of revelation. If faith, as the response to
God's invitation, comes first and the attempt to formulate

it in human words comes second and is dependent on the particular circumstances of language and culture and society of the time, then one common faith can be expressed in many ways. In this context, infallibility must be redefined. If there is only one right answer, and other answers are wrong, then infallibility means someone is guaranteed to have the right answer. But if there are several right answers, then infallibility means something a little different. It might be explained as a guarantee that with one particular formulation a belief is solidly within the common Christian tradition, though there would also have been other ways of expressing the matter.

With this sort of explanation, infallibility would not mean that a formulation, once made, could never be changed again. It would mean it could be rethought and restated by the same channels by which it came about in the first place, though future generations should respect the words already used. It would also mean that where the Catholic Church has traditionally used one way of expressing a Christian doctrine, other explanations used by Protestant and Orthodox Churches are not necessarily wrong. They may simply be expressing the same Christian faith from the point of view of a different language, and culture, and society.

In fact, as Father Küng points out, dogmas solemnly defined by the Church in the past have sometimes been brought up and discussed again (e.g., the different accounts of the Holy Spirit given by the Western and Eastern Churches which were discussed at the Council of Florence). As long as the Church is alive, and as long as believing Christians try to live out the implications of their faith in their own time, place, and circumstances, there will be new understanding and new ways of expressing even those tenets of Christian faith already solemnly defined as dogmas. Jesus once said to some very religious and observant people that the Sabbath (so solemnly declared by the highest authority, speaking on behalf of God) is for man, and not man for the Sabbath. In the same way he would surely say to people worried over dogmatic formulations, that these formulas are for believers, to sustain their faith, rather than the faith of believers being for the sake of continuing the formulations of dogma intact.

This question of our freedom to reopen discussion on matters solemnly and infallibly defined is very important today. It is important because too many Catholics no longer find that the dogmatic formulations sustain them in a life of faith in their present form. It is also important because it is a prerequisite for any serious efforts in ecumenism among the Christian churches. It is important, finally, because we are not true to the gospel unless we retain our power to communicate with non-Christian peoples and to give them a living witness with living explanations of what the gospel and faith in Jesus Christ mean to us in terms of the world in which we live together with these non-Christian peoples.

FOUR

How Should We Explain the Eucharist?

MATTHIAS SCHEEBEN, EDWARD
SCHILLEBEECKX, DUTCH THEOLOGIANS

The last chapter concluded that believers must continue to search for new and appropriate ways of expressing faith in words. Even when a dogma is officially formulated, it does not mean that the quest is ended. Man's experience continues to grow and change, and his understanding of himself and the world continues to grow and change. Each dogmatic formulation is made in terms of the understanding that men have at that time, and in terms of the kind of language and vocabulary that they are using at that time.

Perhaps the clearest example of this for Catholics today is the doctrine of the Eucharist. It is the central sacrament that brings the Church together and makes it a reality in the world. It is supposed to be the great sign and means of unity for Christians. As we know it today, however, it has come to be something that divides the Christian denominations, because although we should be united in Christ, we do not communicate in one another's churches.

What divides us is not really the celebration of the Eucharist itself, but the explanations that the denominations give of it in their official theologies. We Catholics have had, since the Council of Trent, a clearly formulated doctrine which most Protestants vehemently reject, and which is beginning to cause difficulties for increasing numbers of Catholics. The problem is not with the central message that Christ is present to us in the Eucharist. The problem is with the words that are used to describe this presence which are drawn from Aristotelian philosophy, because this philosophy no longer fits our experience of the world.

Actually the philosophical explanations given at Trent are not the only ones the Church has held. The Eucharist has been explained in many different ways in the past. The problem arises only because for some time theologians in the Catholic Church seemed to assume that the Church had intended at Trent to link the truth of the Eucharist to the truth of Aristotelian philosophy, and that this linkage could never be changed. Now even the historians are telling us that this could hardly have been the intention of the Fathers of the Council of Trent, and theologians are beginning to study the development of the theology of the Eucharist from the beginning of the Church to the present, in the Catholic as well as in the Orthodox and Protestant traditions.

The starting point is, of course, with what the gospels tell us of the Last Supper. Jesus did not give us any theology or explanations. He gave us the action itself and the command to go on doing it. We have been figuring out the explanations ever since, in our own ways, in our own times, in our own languages, and against the background of our own philosophies.

What Jesus did must have looked and felt quite different from our Mass. The disciples were used to Jesus doing things in the style of the Hebrew prophets—saying things in stories, saying things in his actions. They were also accustomed to his observing the Jewish rites with deep devotion, but in startling ways giving these rites new and very personal meanings. That is exactly what happened at the Last Supper.

The occasion took place not in a place of worship but in a home. On the other hand, the context was not just any meal; it was not casual and impromptu at all, but was a very sacred occasion. The Jews are accustomed to home liturgy for the Passover. In it they commemorate the liberation of the people of Israel from Egypt, but it is a great deal more than a memorial. It is a re-enactment of the reality, which is, in one sense, the same because through all ages they are sharing the same experience of God's intervention. In another sense it is always new, every time it is celebrated, because it is a present and living reality for these people. In the celebration they transcend time, and experience the unity of the people of Israel gathered into unity in God's covenant.

Jesus was evidently celebrating the Passover meal in this spirit. To make it fully genuine as his personal celebration, he had to put into it his whole existence at that moment in all the dimensions of his experience. He knew he had challenged the authorities beyond endurance, and it had to mean the end of his life. His experience at that moment was primarily the anticipation of his death and his overwhelming desire that other men should find their personal Exodus, their personal Passover or liberation, in that death. He knew that he had come to the threshold of death innocently, because of his passionate proclamation of the Father's will. Therefore he considered his death as a sacrifice, an offering to God which would bring reconciliation with men. He thought of this Passover celebration as a sacrificial meal in a quite special sense.

Jesus blessed and broke bread and gave it to them to eat, in a typical prophetic gesture, prophesying that his body was to be broken for their life. He poured and blessed wine, and gave it to them to drink, again in a prophetic gesture, saying that his blood was to be shed for their life.

When the young Church assembled after the Resurrection experience, what its members recalled was that Jesus had done these things on the eve of his death and had told them to keep doing them in memory of him. Paul said that they should keep celebrating the Lord's death by this action until he came again. Of course, like the Jews in the celebration of the Passover, they knew the action was much more than a memorial.

At this time no one had set up any rubrics or canon law that defined exactly what was to be considered a Eucharist and what was not a Eucharist. We do have very strong evidence, for instance in the document known as the *Didache*, that although sometimes an officially ordained or appointed minister presided at a Eucharist, sometimes other people who had not been ordained, presided at Eucharists because they felt moved by a prophetic spirit. We also know that for many centuries there was a good deal of spontaneity and improvising, with a gradual trend toward certain local patterns.

With the peace of Constantine in the fourth century, the Church became more or less established as the official state religion. Before this time, home liturgies had been the pattern. Now there were far too many people involved, for when one holds a meeting of the whole town, it has to be held in the town hall or some large place. The liturgy was now being celebrated normally in basilicas, and all sorts of customs, ceremonies, and manners of the Byzantine court were introduced. Yet this was not a worldly place or time. It was a place and time of the greatest solemnity, where earth and heaven met and people were momentarily swept up into the mystery. The style of celebration of this period is the style that the Orthodox and other Eastern Churches have retained.

In the Western Church, through the course of the centuries, the focus of attention in the celebration was less and less on the community participation in the worship and the sacrificial meal, and moved more and more toward the things that concretely formed the center of the celebration : the bread and wine. This was probably due to the fact that the people lost touch with the language of the celebration—both the words, which the Western liturgies now had in Latin, and the language of gesture and symbolic action, on which the Eucharistic celebration had always rested. Whatever its causes, the change of focus had unfortunate consequences, for people were more concerned about moving from altar to altar to look at the elevated host than they were concerned with communicating. They also expected results and favors to follow from this looking, beliefs which had more to do with magic than with faith.

The Protestant reformers were very grieved by this state of affairs. They endeavored to recapture some of the Biblical simplicity of the beginnings of the Church, to emphasize again the fellowship meal that had been such a strong feature of the home liturgies of the early Church. In emphasizing the fellowship meal, they tended to de-emphasize or deny the sacrificial character of the action. They also objected to those explanations of the presence of Jesus in the action which focused on the change in the bread and wine, isolated from the happening in the community.

The statements of the Council of Trent and the reforms of Pope Pius V eliminated many of the abuses by prescribing rather strict rubrics. Yet the theology of the Eucharist of the Council of Trent was so preoccupied with refuting the Protestant positions that it really only stated what were considered to be the necessary corrections, rather than presenting a well-rounded and complete explanation.

On account of this preoccupation, the officials of the Catholic Church had little time or energy to consider the very important protests that the Reformers had raised. In the nineteenth century, however, mainly under the auspices of the Benedictine Order, slow, massive, and painstaking studies were undertaken in the history and theology of the liturgy, and in the twentieth century these studies simply exploded into a popular movement among Catholics.

As a result of this movement, when the Church assembled at Vatican II, not only theologians and liturgical specialists, but many thinking Catholics realized that for the Mass to become vitally meaningful to the masses of the faithful again, the Church needed to change the rite considerably and to broaden the theology by picking up again all those elements that had slipped out of the picture. Because there had been practically no changes in either the pattern of celebration or the official theological explanations in the 400 years since Trent, this changing of the rite is proving difficult—for one reason, because some people assumed that if there had been no change in 400 years, it meant that everything was fully developed and should never change again.

Looking at the problem with the longer perspective of 2000 years, one sees not only the development of the rite of celebration as sketched above, but also a corresponding theological development. One can see clearly that the explanations of the Eucharist the Christians gave at each stage arose out of their experience of what they were actually doing in the celebration.

In the patristic times, the theory of the Eucharist was mainly concerned with the unity that was being celebrated. By gathering for the Eucharist the Christians were proclaiming that they were of one heart and soul, and were pledging themselves to keep striving after unity. Occasionally, the Fathers of the Church mentioned the change of the bread and wine, but they were not concerned with how it happened, nor at what precise moment. The focus of attention was on the whole action of celebration and the community that participated in it. The theology therefore, was more about the change that should take

place in the congregation than about the change in the
bread and wine, though the Fathers did rather casually
use some words like transfiguration and transformation.
When the experience of the faithful in the Eucharistic
celebration began to focus more on the host as an object to
be looked at, the people were, of course, more interested in
knowing at exactly what moment the change happened.
Moreover, the theologians, perhaps without realizing it,
were drawn into an almost exclusive preoccupation with
what happened to the things of the celebration and just
how it happened. This is how Catholics were given a Eucharistic theology in terms of "transubstantiation." The
word could be taken in the same sense of mystery that had
been preserved in earlier terms like transfiguration and
transformation. Most Catholics in the last few centuries
were probably taught the word "transubstantiation" without any reference to its meaning in Aristotelian philosophy. For them, transubstantiation meant just thinking of
the mystery of Christ's presence with us—a religious,
rather than a philosophical, meaning.

The problem arose only where transubstantiation was
interpreted as a philosophical word. Some theologians and
thoughtful people outside the Catholic Church really
thought that one could not be a Catholic believer without
accepting the Aristotelian view of matter as the one true
explanation of the universe. Such people also tried to teach
this philosophical explanation to ordinary Catholics who
had never had any questions about substance and accidents,
and who did not want to be philosophers anyway.

In the nineteenth century, about the time of Vatican I,
a German Catholic theologian, Matthias Scheeben, wrote
a book entitled *The Mysteries of Christianity*. In it, he
insisted that the Eucharist could only be explained at all
if one realizes that it is a mystery; that is, a very special
kind of truth. The characteristic of mysteries, according
to Scheeben, is that they are not matters that we find out

for ourselves by observation, but truths given us as a special gift from God. In addition, he said, mysteries can never be explained in words and concepts that really, fully, and immediately correspond to the reality they represent. We can only be told about a mystery through an analogy, that is, by a comparison, because the reality is beyond our experience and, therefore, beyond our language.

Like St. Thomas Aquinas, Scheeben saw the Eucharist as the gathering that constitutes the Church. He suggested that we shall understand it better, not when we try to separate the different components and analyze what makes them work, but, rather, when we try to see how the Eucharist links with all the other great mysteries of faith into one whole vision of the meaning of life.

In our own time, theologians have been trying to do just this. They have asked themselves why we come together to celebrate the Eucharist, what fruits we hope to receive from it, and how we can link this mystery with our traditional explanations in a continuity of faith.

In the Netherlands there has been some especially good teamwork among theologians and catechists. They have tried to discover, in terms of the way most people think about the world and themselves today, what would be the best way to interpret the traditional doctrines to them. These theologians have published a *New Catholic Catechism for Adults*, which has brought new inspiration and insights to a great many Catholics who found that their questions were not being answered in the doctrine they had learned before. Outstanding in this group of theologians is Edward Schillebeeckx, a Belgian Dominican who teaches at the university of Nijmegen, and has written a book called *The Eucharist*.

Over a period of years, before and during the Second Vatican Council, these theologians carried on an exchange of views, scholarship, and insight in professional journals. What came of their exchange is expressed in the terms

"transfinalization" and "transignification." Briefly, they
say that when one looks back over the celebration and explanation of the Eucharist by the Christian community,
what is important is the presence of the risen Christ in a
concrete and immediate way in the midst of the assembled
faithful, uniting them to form the reality of the Church in
the world. This presence is expressed in a community action in which the president of the assembly takes bread and
wine as Jesus did, and pronounces over them the words of
Jesus, "This is my body; this is my blood." The action is
only complete when the offerings are consumed, as a sign
of unity and faith.

In the action, what was simply bread before changes its
meaning, that is, changes what it really is, to the bodily
presence of Christ in his sacrificial death and resurrection,
which he invites the worshipers to share. It is the fundamental reality of the bread which changes, not its chemical
composition, nor what constitutes it physically. The fundamental reality of the bread is what makes bread bread
and not something else. If you stop to think about it, it is
rather difficult to figure out exactly what makes bread
bread. It is not what it is made of, because bread can be
made of wheat, rye, barley, or other cereals; it can be
leavened or unleavened, dark or light; it comes in large
loaves or small rolls, and in all sorts of different shapes.
What really makes bread bread is the purpose for which
man uses it, and the meaning it has for him, that is, what
it does for him. What bread *is* is only partly explained in
terms of nourishment, and largely in terms of culture and
society. In terms of biological nourishment, there is absolutely no difference between unconsecrated and consecrated
bread, but in terms of the human meaning and purpose of
this bread, there is all the difference that there could possibly be.

It is important to remember Scheeben's admonition that
this is in the realm of mystery, where the best words we

can possibly find are still not really apt for the reality. With that admonition in mind, it is helpful to realize that when the Dutch theologians speak of transfinalization, they mean that because the bread's purpose has changed, it changes the whole human reality of the bread. When they speak of transignification, they say that because the bread's meaning has changed, its fundamental reality is different.

What is especially helpful about the Dutch theologians' explanation is that you cannot understand it in any way that does not draw the community right into the action and right into the change. You cannot distort the explanation into a more or less magical one in which people might expect grace and salvation to happen to them and in them without their getting in any way personally involved.

Soon after these discussions and proposals for contemporary explanations of the Eucharist became public, Pope Paul VI issued an encyclical called *Mysterium fidei,* in which he praised these endeavors and the attempt to provide people with a genuine contemporary spirituality built around the Eucharist. He said in this encyclical that he thought that the word transubstantiation should still be used in conjunction with the words transfinalization and transignification to make quite sure that no one would think that such an important aspect of the doctrine had simply been dropped.

It appears that the Pope saw some danger that people would begin to think about the Eucharist as simply a memorial, depending for its reality and its meaning on human initiative. He wanted to make it very clear that we are invited to an encounter in which God offers Himself to us through our unity in the personal presence of Jesus extended to us across the centuries. The Pope's personal judgment was that for most adult Catholics today the full spiritual meaning of the Eucharist is carried in the word transubstantiation. Many theologians hope, because the word is still so offensive to devout Protestant Christians, and because younger Catholics are quite confused by it, that one day it will slide out of the official formulations into history, along with transfiguration and transformation, as just one way of describing an elusive and many-faceted mystery.

FIVE

Who Is Jesus Christ?

KARL RAHNER, F. X. DURRWELL, EDWARD SCHILLEBEECKX

The discussion in the last chapter begs many questions about the role and person of Jesus of Nazareth. It demands a further question as to the meaning and importance of the death of Jesus, and prompts all sorts of questions about the meaning of the resurrection. Many Catholics reading it may also have been quite disturbed with a presentation in which Jesus is shown to be figuring things out about the meaning of life like any other man.

As with the discussion of the Eucharist, it may be well to begin with the realization that Jesus did not give us a theology of himself. He simply was there, giving people his presence, his friendship, his example, and his preaching about the kingdom and the will of the Father. Moreover, we do not have an objective chronicle of his life and deeds, nor do we have a literal record of his words. We know now that the gospels were written simply as proclamations of the good news of salvation, which the early Christian community had found in the experience of the resurrection, and which they wanted to share with others. They had no intention of giving us a biography of Jesus, which is why so many things seem to be missing in the story, and why the four accounts do not always agree.

The basic message that the apostles preached was that they had had experiences of Jesus as alive and present after his death. These experiences had transformed them, and had transformed the world completely for them; at last everything fitted together, everything made sense. Jesus who was crucified had been raised up again by God, so that in Him all men could be raised up to eternal life. Because of their personal and vivid experiences of the risen Jesus, the apostles began to look back over the Hebrew scriptures with which they had grown up, and to see everything as centering in the person of Jesus, who somehow fulfilled the promises and hopes of all that went before. They proclaimed that he was Christ, that is, the Messiah, the anointed and chosen one who would usher in the promised kingdom in which all men's hopes would be fulfilled and God would reign among men forever. At the same time, they kept preaching that he would come again in glory, because they knew that the messianic times had not yet been fully realized, and that they, the Church, had to strive to fulfill the messianic promises of peace, love, and universal brotherhood among men.

The apostles also began to proclaim that the risen Christ was Lord. They used the Greek word *kyrios*, which the Jews had reserved for God, the Father of all. But they used the word in a context where it was always clear that they were not identifying Jesus with God, the Father of all, but relating him to the Father in a unique and special way.

In later centuries, Christians kept asking questions about that special relationship, and about the title Lord. Again, as with the Eucharist, we are faced with a mystery. We have the living experience of Jesus, and of the risen Christ in the apostolic Church, and we have their testimony of what Jesus meant to them. They gave the testimony in whatever words they could put together, in language that was to them religious, mysterious, and which hinted at more than it said. One thing about their writings is clear: God had been revealed to them in their friendship with Jesus, in a conclusive and overwhelming way.

The Christians who asked questions about Jesus in the early centuries of Christianity asked them against the background of Greek philosophies and religions, against the background of a vision of the universe in which their time and space were somehow contained within eternity and infinity as though these were somewhat like continuations of time and space. They asked their questions against the background of religious references to a world of gods who sometimes descended and mingled with men, intervening in their affairs and then withdrawing again. Of course, their great problem, as well as ours, was to find any way at all to give expression to religious experience and to faith. As was pointed out with reference to Scheeben in the last chapter, no matter what words were used to explain these mysteries, the words are analogies or comparisons that never quite fit.

Gradually, formulations were worked out in that context to answer the questions, and classic expressions of them exist in our great liturgical creeds. The formulation now called the Nicene Creed says it this way:

I believe in one God, the Father almighty. . . .

And I believe in one Lord, Jesus Christ, the only-begotten Son of God, born of the Father before all ages—

God of God, Light of Light, true God of true God—

Begotten, not made, of one substance with the Father, by whom all things were made—

Who for us men and for our salvation came down from heaven, and he became flesh by the Holy Spirit of the Virgin Mary, and was made man.

He was also crucified for us, suffered under Pontius Pilate, and was buried, and on the third day he rose again according to the Scriptures.

He ascended into heaven and sits at the right hand
of the Father.
He will come again in glory to judge the living and
the dead, and of his kingdom there will be no end. . . .

This is a magnificent statement of what Jesus Christ
means to us as Christians. We are so familiar with it from
our Sunday Mass celebration that we may think of it as
quite simple and straightforward. Yet, if you reflect on it
for a while and try to read it as though you had never come
across it before, you will begin to realize that it combines
in a single recital two very different kinds of information.
It tells of Jesus being born of Mary, executed by cruci-
fixion by the authorization of Pontius Pilate, and buried.
This account is given from observation. It could have appeared in a police record, and it could be verified by witnesses.

This recital of observable facts is set within another
very different recital. The second recital says that before
the beginning of all time, Jesus was born in a sort of pre-
time as the only son of God; that at a point in time he
came down from heaven (because before that point he was
up there with the Father) and became man (because before that he was the son of God but he was not human);
that after his death he came alive again and at another
point in time went back up into heaven where he had
come from; that he is now sitting up there beside the Father, waiting to come back down; and that when he
comes it will be gloriously, assembling those who are still
alive and those who have already died, and establishing
an endless kingdom.

The first point to notice about the second recital is that
it is much longer, fuller, more dramatic, whereas the first
is terse and dry. The second point to notice is that it is
composed entirely of assertions that could not possibly
have been checked by observation. Yet, you will notice, it
is written as though these things could have been ob-

served: a story of two persons, one of whom stays always in that upper region while the other moves to and fro between heaven and earth, linking them together in one experience.

Actually, the second recital is written rather like a solemn pageant, a sort of liturgical ceremony embracing all of space and all of time. It becomes clear, when you think about it, that not only could these things never have been observed, but that those who wrote them did not think of them as parallel to the first account, but as a spiritual and religious interpretation of the first account. They did not think Jesus had climbed down from heaven the way he climbed down from Mount Olivet, nor that he sat beside the Father the way he sat beside John at the Last Supper.

If you put the two recitals together and think of them as one, you find that the historical, observable facts provide the immediate experience which the Christian community has always wanted to interpret. The other part is the secondary reflection on that experience, that is, the interpretation. If you realize this, it does not matter that Christian theology through the ages has discussed the mysteries of the life of Christ, treating both layers of the creed on an equal footing. The whole account means that Christians, by their faith commitment see Jesus as illuminating the meaning of all history, all human problems, the whole of existence—as being at the beginning with God, and at the end, and as linking heaven and earth together, that is, reconciling God and man.

Through most of our Christian history this experience was well understood. It is only quite recently that we have begun to ask whether religious statements were "literally" true, meaning verifiable by observation. This is a special and very limited understanding of truth, but our technically-minded age is in grave danger of thinking that such verification is the only criterion of truth. If we should ever give in to this tendency, we would fall into despair, because we would no longer be able to find meaning or value in life.

On account of this modern tendency to ask whether things are "literally" true, Christians of our times have had some new questions about their faith, and theologians have had to reopen the whole discussion of who Jesus is, what his experience of life was, and what his mission in the world was and is. They have also had to ask new questions about the resurrection.

You may have noticed that one item in the Nicene creed's account of Jesus presents a special problem. It is by no means self-evident whether the statement, "and on the third day he rose again," is to be included in the first recital or the second. Some people are quick to point out that even St. Paul said that if Christ is not really risen then all our hopes are in vain. But this begs the question, simply because we do not know whether St. Paul was thinking of the resurrection in the first or second category when he made the remark. We do know that everywhere in the Christian Scriptures, where we have testimonies of the risen Christ, religious mystery language is used—dazzling lights, white garments, appearances sudden as a flash, mysterious inability to recognize him at first, an ecstatic glow of joy with the recognition, a sudden fading away. We also know that the apostles explained that they were unable to get a documentation similar to a modern-day police record—no unbelievers had seen Jesus, and the guards posted at the tomb told a different story than that of the believers.

Father F. X. Durrwell, a Redemptorist theologian who has been much less in the public eye than most of the authors mentioned in this book, has written a very exhaustive study entitled *The Resurrection*. The book does not really solve the mystery of this event, but when you reflect on all that has been put together in this study, you begin to realize that it simply does not matter whether the resurrection belongs in the first or second recital, because the overwhelmingly important thing is that it does hold the two recitals together. The apostles spoke out of a faith experience, one of Jesus alive and present to them, that totally transformed them and transformed the world for them. The evidence that they presented for the truth of their proclamation was their own life, hope, and joy, and the living experience of the community of love and trust. Because they never asked the question whether the resurrection was true as a naturally observable phenomenon, it never occurred to them to answer the question either, and because they never asked or answered it, we shall never know.

Meanwhile, contemporary theologians have been grappling with a different but closely related problem. When the second recital in the creed calls Jesus Lord and only-begotten Son of God, it is careful to underscore that it is speaking the language of mystery by adding the words ''God of God, Light of Light, true God of true God.'' This should be a signal to any deeply religious person not to manipulate these words as though they were chemical formulae or mathematical equations. They are simply hints of a reality that eludes us, which we can describe in various rather poetic or picturesque ways, but which we can never grasp.

Perhaps we have at times overstepped the bounds in our speculations because some of the accounts we have of Jesus take for granted the fact that He was God and existed before all ages. According to these accounts, the only problem is to figure out how exactly Jesus could be truly human.

This is, of course, quite upside-down, as has been pointed out in a complicated but very effective way by Karl Rahner, who has already appeared in Chapters I and III. In several lengthy essays in the collection of his works entitled *Theological Investigations*, Rahner has discussed our understanding of Jesus Christ. He has pointed out that theology is really never the study of God, but rather the

study of man and his experience of God, because that experience is all that is really accessible to us. When we are
considering Jesus, our experience, and that of the whole
Christian tradition, is that of a man in whose human existence we have glimpsed the invisible God whose only
image is man. In the experience of the man Jesus, and most
especially in the way He met His death and in His triumph
over death, we have met the image of God who gives life
and gives Himself, in a shocking, startlingly clear and
unique way, once and for all.

In order to understand the revelation that we have received in Jesus Christ, it is important to realize that man
is the image of God, not in some objectively, externally
visible way, but in the depth of his experience as he looks
in on himself and shares himself with others. If we were
to think of Jesus as the hollow shell of a man with a divine
inside, we would have scooped out the real channel of divine revelation, which is the human inside. Very painstakingly, Rahner has been busy rediscovering the human
inside of Jesus—his gradually-emerging consciousness of
himself, his ordinary human effort to learn, understand,
and interpret, his ordinary human feelings about friendship and loneliness, loyalty and betrayal, life and death,
patriotism and the acknowledgment of the common destiny of all men.

Jesus learned to speak, to think, to pray, and to figure
out the will of the Father from the Hebrew Scriptures,
from the faith of those around him, and from what was
happening in the world. He tried out his prophetic mission
in different ways, and, by trial and error, followed through
with the ones that seemed to serve his goals best. He began to realize that the price of his prophetic proclamations of God's judgment, as he understood it, would be
eventual arrest and execution. He chose to stand his
ground and continue his proclamation. He prayed about it
and reflected on it, and came to see his forthcoming death

as an innocent sacrifice for the lives of others.

Many people have asked questions about the consciousness of Jesus: how it could be the consciousness of God and man at the same time, whether the divine and the human knowledge were mixed together and blended into one, or whether they were separate streams of consciousness in which just a few items of information were allowed to trickle through from the divine to the human layer when they were needed for his mission.

It will be evident from what has been discussed that these are simply misconceived questions. First of all, God does not think conceptually. Nor does God "know" the way human persons know, because when we speak of God as a person, we are using an analogy. We really mean something more like "beyond personality." God is a deep mystery, and it is utterly presumptuous to talk of God's way of knowing as though we could ever find out what that way might be. Secondly, when we speak of Jesus as being human, we know exactly what we mean, but when we speak of Jesus as being divine we really do not know what we mean. We know that we do not mean a simple equation like "Mrs. Jones is the former Susan Smith," precisely because God is more beyond personhood than simply person.

If we could not say anything more positive than this, we would be in a very difficult position. Father Edward Schillebeeckx, who was introduced in the last chapter, has tried to express our understanding of the divinity of Jesus in a way that would explain it best to people of our time. In his book *Christ the Sacrament of the Encounter with God*, he tries to understand and preserve the fundamental meaning of the apostles' proclamation that Jesus is Lord, and of the creedal declaration that he is the only-begotten Son born of the Father before all ages.

Like Rahner, Schillebeeckx begins from the assumption that we know exactly what we mean when we say that

Jesus is man, and that in our experience of Jesus as man we have come to an understanding that he is divine. Schillebeeckx explains this understanding not as though we could grasp reality *beyond* our experience, but because we can meet reality *in* our experience. Jesus is the "sacrament" of our meeting with God. We cannot meet God as God, because God is transcendent, which really means unmeetable or unencounterable. What the apostles told us was that to meet Jesus was such an experience that it was to be invited to an immediate personal encounter with the invisible and untouchable God, because of what Jesus was. In Him, in a unique way, people were and are brought into contact with God so that this contact transforms their whole being. He is the place of encounter with God—He is divine.

SIX

What Difference Does Grace Make?

TEILHARD DE CHARDIN, HENRI DE LUBAC, KARL RAHNER

You may have noticed a tendency in this book, and elsewhere in current writings about theology, to explain everything religious in the most natural, everyday, and ordinary ways. There seems to be less special religious or theological language, and less of an idea of separate sacred and secular areas in our lives.

This tendency is largely the result of something that has been called secularization, the general idea of which was hinted at in the first chapter of this book. In the course of the ages man has taken more and more possession of the earth and all that is in and around it. He can control and understand much more than could people of past ages. He even has a far better understanding of himself. Today, for instance, man realizes that the customs, rules, and ideas of propriety and beauty in his society are not always shared by other societies. These customs are not the inevitable and only right way of doing things.

When men understood less of how things worked in the world and in society, they tended to see the transcendent God as a powerful organizer of the universe who was manipulating everything behind the scenes. This God made thunder when he was angry, sent plagues and disasters when he thought he should punish people, and redressed in another world the balance of everything that went wrong and worked unjustly in this world. He worked in ways that could not be seen. Outwardly, a man might seem to be good and righteous, but inwardly he could have lost God's grace and be living in darkness. Outwardly there might be no difference in a person before and after he was baptized or absolved in the sacrament of penance, but inwardly there might be all the difference between night and day in that special realm where God operated, which was always inaccessible to man's experience.

As men began to take control of more of the world, they also tended to take more of the responsibility for what was going on. This responsibility applied, of course, to the external world. There we now tend to have lightning conductors which take the place of a man making the sign of the cross during storms. We have inspection provisions and air traffic controllers instead of prayers for travelers. We construct irrigation systems and seed clouds from the air instead of holding processions and novenas for rain. But this responsibility is applied also in the inner world of our psychic or spiritual life. Here we have begun to be distrustful of ritual ways of gaining God's favor. We have reasoned that a person cannot receive an infusion of additional charity and grace unless he is really loving more and living more.

This line of thinking has led most Catholic theologians and other thoughtful persons much further than they had at first realized that they were going to travel in their revolution of ideas. The accounts of the spiritual life of Christians, the redemptive work of Christ, and the "plus value" of the Church have begun to sound more like common sense psychology than like strictly Christian teaching. More recently some people have begun to have an uneasy feeling that some modern Catholic writers are doing away with the ideas of grace and the supernatural life entirely.

Accusations to this effect were made, for instance, against a very important contemporary writer who was not really a theologian. Pierre Teilhard de Chardin was a French Jesuit scientist who specialized in archaeology. He was very interested in the theory of evolution and the various ways it might be tested by present observations of what remains we have of the earliest times from tool-using and more or less man-like beings. Because Teilhard was a deeply religious man, he had a great drive to integrate what he was discovering from the natural sciences with his understanding of salvation in Christ.

Teilhard had meditated a good deal on the theology in the letters of St. Paul and on what some of the Fathers of the Church had developed from St. Paul's remarks. From these sources he developed a magnificent, sweeping vision of the universe and all of history with Christ running through it as a sort of axis, making sense and unity of it all. He saw creation, redemption, and salvation all woven together in the same unified process of evolution.

According to Teilhard's theory, during the course of the ages, inanimate (dead) matter is drawn into such complex patterns that it develops an inner spontaneity and there is a breakthrough to living beings. At a further stage there is a breakthrough to reflexive self-awareness, that is, to human beings. After this stage the process of evolution becomes conscious, because men know and project the goals they are striving for and the changes they are trying to make. Looking forward, one can anticipate that the next breakthrough must be an immense unity of all mankind bound together in a network of relationships of knowledge and love. The breakthrough to that great unification, Teilhard calls the Omega Point.

He then makes a bold suggestion, no longer as a scientist but as a Christian believer, that we have a preview of Omega Point: that the whole world is being drawn toward the second coming of Jesus Christ in glory; that this second coming will be the breakthrough; and that the break-

through will be the outcome of the central strand of evolution which is the Church, because Jesus is already within
history which is consciously striving towards its fulfillment. He links this suggestion together with the Pauline
idea, which appears in the creed quoted in the last chapter,
that all things were made in Jesus Christ. Jesus is, so to
speak, the model or pattern of the world from the very
beginning. The ultimate goal of evolution is the ''christi-
fication'' of the whole world.

In this very beautiful scheme, which appears in *The
Phenomenon of Man* but which you may find more readable
in *The Divine Milieu*, nature and grace, the natural and
the supernatural, are continuous within one harmonious
whole. When these ideas first came into circulation they
raised great concern because they sounded at first as
though they contradicted the basic Christian teaching that
God's self-gift to man is not a necessity of man's nature
but utterly free and completely beyond what men are naturally capable of striving after.

Teilhard de Chardin was primarily a scientist rather
than a theologian. Some professional theologians, however,
also were reflecting on the same questions. Foremost among
them was a very close personal friend of Teilhard, also a
French Jesuit, Henri de Lubac. A great scholar in the
writings of the early Fathers of the Church, Henri de
Lubac wrote a book called *The Supernatural*, which was
much misunderstood and criticized at first, but since then
has been quite generally accepted. Many years later he
wrote another book on the same topic called *The Mystery
of the Supernatural*, in which he answers his critics care-
fully, thoughtfully, and at length.

Father de Lubac's research into the history of the idea
of the supernatural was immense, but the ideas that resulted from it were quite simple. The history, as usual, is a
history of many generations trying to explain things in
terms of their contemporary ways of thought and their

own experience of life. In the Hebrew scriptures the relationship between God and men was described sometimes in terms of covenant or reciprocally binding duties and sometimes as sheer favor shown by God. Whatever God was bound to was always the result of his promise, of his having bound himself. The Jewish idea of the covenant of God and man always looks back to creation itself as the original setting up of the covenant, however; so that it appears as if simply by creating men, God has already bound himself to bring them into his friendship.

In the Christian Scriptures, we are told, especially by Paul and Luke, that God showers his favors freely on all, but on different people in different ways. It is clear that no one has any claim to a particular gift such as prophecy. The apostolic writers, however, seem to assume that God is eagerly waiting to bestow salvation itself on everybody, through the preaching of the gospel of Christ.

It seems that from the second century to the time of St. Augustine, in the early fifth century, the teachers in the Church felt a great burden to defend the freedom of God in salvation against those who emphasized self-perfection by sheer human moral effort. In fact, St. Augustine, when confronted with a heretic known as Pelagius, put such heavy emphasis on the initiative of God in the salvation of men that many people reading him began to wonder where and how man's freedom came into the picture at all. Among the medieval theologians, St. Anselm, writing in the eleventh century, felt he had to redress the balance by re-emphasizing the freedom of man.

Peter the Lombard, in the twelfth century, wrote of grace as being simply the indwelling of the Holy Spirit. This emphasized the initiative of God, but it should, of course, be considered in terms of the human response and disposition that make the indwelling of God's Spirit (God's breath of life) in a person possible. This must have been what St. Thomas Aquinas had in mind, writing in the thirteenth century, when he disagreed with Peter the Lombard and insisted that grace is a supernatural habit of the soul. Habit, in this instance, meant disposition or way of being. Duns Scotus, toward the end of the same century, said that grace is the supernatural habit of charity, that is, that grace is a loving disposition.

Up to that time, it seems clear that theologians were observing the Christian experience and theorizing from it. There are a few problems connected with the way they were slipping in the word supernatural, and these problems became steadily more complicated and developed into centuries-long debates. In these debates it was no longer a question of observing Christian experience and reflecting on it in order to explain itself. It began to be much more of a logic game within the word-system they had adopted.

A key figure in this debate was Cardinal Cajetan, a famous sixteenth century commentator on the writings of Thomas Aquinas. In order to complete and systematize the whole logical pattern, Cajetan made grace and the supernatural into a sort of separate and independent world that hardly ever impinged on the natural or the realm of creation. Even though Thomas had said that man is made in the image of God and desires, therefore, with his whole being to see God, Cajetan said that Thomas could not have meant a natural desire arising from the way man is made.

If it was not a natural desire, however, the explanations were going to get very complicated. On the one hand, there now had to be all sorts of special ''actual'', graces to set the process going, and they all had to come from a special world outside the world of experiences. On the other hand, there also had to be an explanation of how the world of ''pure nature'' would work if grace did not come into it, and what man's goals would then be.

What resulted is what theologians have sometimes called a two-story universe, one in which two separate layers never really mingle. One story is the layer of the world of experience, in which we know what is happening; the other is the world of the supernatural or of grace, where all kinds of things may be happening which never register in human experience. Most of what we were taught in the Baltimore Catechism for instance, followed this scheme of Cajetan in relation to grace, to the effects of the sacraments, faith, and many other topics. It is unfortunate that many Catholics have grown up with the impression that this gives them the whole traditional teaching of the Church. As Henri de Lubac demonstrated, it did not even give them the teaching of Thomas Aquinas correctly.

Father de Lubac pointed out that Thomas had been misinterpreted and had really seen nature and grace in a much more unified way. The idea of "pure nature" is not very helpful, because all we know is that no such thing ever existed. The whole Judaeo-Christian tradition insists that from the very beginning God, in fact, intends man to come into an intimate friendship with him. Moreover, this imaginary idea of pure nature is actually obstructive because it suggests that the grace of God is unnecessary for a perfect human life. In this way it seems to contradict that very need for God's grace that it is trying to safeguard.

What is really important is to hold to the understanding that God's grace is necessary for everyone. It is redemptive, healing grace in a disrupted world in which we have never seen anyone attaining ultimate natural happiness by human efforts not dependent on God's healing intervention. This granted, we are ready to ask questions about how our natural efforts and experiences are related to that grace which God bestows.

Karl Rahner has probably given the clearest answers to these questions in two essays entitled *Nature and Grace,* one of which is published as a book, and the other, more complicated one, is published in the collection *Theological*

Investigations. Rahner makes two main points. The first is that in the historical situation in which we find ourselves, we have been called by God to a life of grace. This call applies to all men everywhere, and we should not waste our time speculating about some imaginary human beings who might have existed without being called to grace. Since these ''pure nature'' people do not, did not, and will not exist, they can neither concern us in any way nor enlighten us about our existence.

The second point is that, if grace has any meaning at all, it is God's invitation working at the very core of human existence, at the roots of man's being. That means grace works through man's humanness, his spontaneity and creativeness, his ability to think and take possession of his own being and make his own decisions. But in that case, grace cannot be a completely separate realm from the realm of experience. It can only be a change in the way man experiences his whole life, the way he thinks, feels, and decides. In other words, the supernatural cannot be regarded as beyond consciousness because if it were, it would make no sense; it would be subnatural rather than supernatural.

Grace is God's personal love for man and the human response to it. But no one makes a human response of love which is entirely outside the realm of his conscious existence. With the reflection that we have to recall the important explanations in terms of ''uncreated grace,'' Rahner points out that although we have a noun for grace, it is not a thing at all. It is not a substance, or a sort of fluid, or an electric current that God communicates; he communicates himself in friendship. Whatever is changed in the human person by grace is the result of that friendship, which mellows and transforms him and opens up all kinds of possibilities that were hidden before.

It is not necessary to suppose that God's offer of friendship is communicated in an extra-sensory way that is totally outside the realm of experience. It is communicated by the happening of Jesus in the world, and by the community of believers that extends that happening through history and throughout society, and by the special moments of celebration, which we call the sacraments, in which the happening of the presence of Jesus so particularly comes about.

If, then, we ask what difference grace really makes, the answer is that it makes all the difference in the world to everything and everybody. But if we ask someone to point out exactly what are the effects of grace in a situation, and what are the results of natural effort alone, the answer is that it is not a sensible question. Grace is not parallel to nature, but transforms and sustains it, and focuses it on its real goals. Everything that is a work of grace is also a work of nature, and there is simply no way of separating them and looking at them one at a time in a given situation.

SEVEN

Have We Forgotten Original Sin?

ANDRE-MARIE DUBARLE, PIET SCHOONENBERG

The reason that grace is absolutely necessary for a good life and for the salvation of each human person is clear. The world in which we live is not one that helps everyone to lead a good life. This world is quite seriously disrupted with wars, class struggles, crimes of violence, crimes of fraud and deceit, racial injustices, and a pervading distrust. Many people in our world feel unwanted and unnoticed, perhaps even rejected by the society that gave them their existence. There are times for even the most fortunate among us when we feel that our whole being is set at cross purposes with the universe.

Men cannot redeem themselves from this sense of frustration or from the destructive and self-defeating situations that cause the frustration. They cannot redeem themselves from it because their own human resources are shaped and limited by what society has given them and done for them, and the point is precisely that this falls short of what is needed. Salvation, or redemption, must come from God because it must come from a greater source of being and of healing power.

This is why all the religions of the world speak of redemption, in one vocabulary or another. They all indicate the need and the promise of a liberation in which people

are set free from a general frustration of purpose in the
human condition. Christian tradition teaches that Jesus
Christ offers to all men that redemption and reconciliation
with God their Father, and with one another, which they
so desperately need. Christian teaching has usually worked
backward from the redemption offered in Jesus to the need
for that redemption.

We have labeled that need for redemption "original
sin." Because Catholics have sometimes been taught a
rather shallow concept of original sin, in recent times many
people have found it difficult to accept the doctrine. They
believe that the doctrine of original sin obliges them to
feel guilty about some mysterious offense committed long
ago by two people who were the first man and woman, and
on whose account all human persons ever since have been
punished by God with difficulties, misfortunes, and the
general frustration of everything that they feel life should
be. People who think that this is what the doctrine means
usually have a sneaking feeling (which they may be unable to admit to themselves) that the whole thing is unfair
and that it is really God who ought to feel guilty about it.

Obviously, there is a misunderstanding somewhere. Careful study reveals that there are several misunderstandings.
They are concerned with the interpretation of the Scripture stories about Adam and Eve, with the understanding
of the nature of sin and its effects, and with the understanding of the kind of personal responsibility that is involved.

The first misunderstanding is one that relates to our
reading of Scripture in many other instances besides original sin. If we read the story of Adam and Eve as
though it were a chronicle of what happened at the beginning of human history, we are reading into it something that the original narrators never intended at all.
They wrote in a style and pattern which tells us their
purpose was to light up the meaning of the human situ-

ation, not in the past but in the present. They tell a classic type of story that relates not how things were at the beginning, but the meaning and explanation of how things are now. Adam, or man, and Eve, or the mother of the living, are brought into being by God in his image. Their being is whole, complete, integrated; it makes sense; it "adds up." But they sin, and one sin leads to another, and we have the recital of the sins of one generation after another of their descendants, all becoming tangled in the sinful situation of the race.

Paul, in his letter to the Romans, knew the story meant just that. He referred to this story to explain his understanding of the role of Christ in the world. He said that as in Adam all have sinned, so in Christ all are reconciled. He spoke of Christ as the second Adam. The unity of mankind, represented by the Adam in the story of the beginning, has been broken by sin, but it is to be restored in Jesus Christ who is to be the new Adam, the new man, the end of all things. Jesus is presented as a new beginning of trust and reconciliation in whom all mankind can be reconstructed into a community of harmony—peace among men and peace with God. The second coming of Jesus is set up as a kind of climax at the end of time in which all human possibilities are to be realized.

John the evangelist picked up another strain from the Hebrew Scriptures. He emphasized the superhuman power and complexity of sin when he referred to the devil or Satan as the adversary against whom Jesus contends. For John, Jesus is the light that shines into a darkened world where people are no longer able to see things clearly because the powers of darkness have been at work obscuring the reality. In none of the Hebrew or Christian Scriptures, however, can you find a clearcut distinction between personal sin and original sin. The Scriptures suggest that one will not find a perfectly innocent man because, living in a situation of sin, we become personally entangled in it.

The second misunderstanding in the doctrine of original sin is concerned with what sin, in general, is and what its effects are. Sin is not simply the disobeying of arbitrary commands called out by God and punished by penalties arbitrarily selected by God. Sin is, rather, a break with the right order and harmony of God's world, which sets things awry in it and complicates life for everybody. To strike another is to arouse anger and evoke a whole chain of violent acts. To be unfaithful in one marriage is to cause a faint, diffuse anxiety in all marriages. To cheat or defraud or betray a secret even once is to start ripples of fear and distrust through the whole society.

It is not some arbitrary edict of God that people should pay the penalty for the sin of those who lived before them. It is because of the way we are constituted that our lives are so largely shaped by those who have lived before. As individuals, we are not made out of nothing, but out of history. We profit from the goodness of those who went before and we suffer from their failures.

The result of this is that no one really starts with a clean slate. To achieve a full, good human life, we need the ever-new intervention of God's saving grace in our lives. This leads to the third misunderstanding about original sin. People find that they cannot possibly feel guilty or consider themselves to blame for something that others have done. Actually, though, they are not expected to feel guilty or to accept the blame.

Although the official teachings of the Church, for instance Canon 5 of the Council of Trent's teachings on original sin, have used the Latin words *reus* and *reatus,* which we translate as "guilty" and "guilt," this should be understood in context.

The Latin terms were originally taken from the courts, and referred to the defendant even before the trial. He was responsible in the sense of being "answerable." He had to give an account of himself with respect to the accusation. This is somewhat different from the way we use the term, because today when a person is called guilty, we assume that the verdict has been given that he is blameworthy.

A more correct interpretation would be that all men together and each person individually must accept responsibility for the complex of sin in the world—that is, each man must accept the obligation to do something about it. But each man is only obliged to accept the blame for those things that he himself has put out of order.

In contemporary Catholic theology, some people have been concerned that this interpretation seems to contradict the official teaching of the Church, and therefore to sweep the real concept of original sin out of the way. The history and formulation of the theology of sin is quite complicated, and it is not easy to evaluate this charge without much study. Two contemporary theologians have been particularly helpful in undertaking and publishing such studies. The first is the Dominican Scripture scholar André-Marie Dubarle, who first published his study in France in 1958, and in 1964 published an enlarged and revised English edition, *The Biblical Doctrine of Original Sin*. The second is the Dutch Jesuit theologian, Piet Schoonenberg, who has summarized some of his extensive historical and theological studies in a book called *Man and Sin*.

Father Dubarle points out that nowhere does the Bible use the term "original sin." This is really a theological idea that developed in the course of the ages. The important question from the point of view of a biblical scholar is which developments of this theology seem to be in harmony with Scripture.

The basic scriptural idea is that of the "sin of the world," the general entanglement of mankind in sin, which makes a wall of resistance to the entry of God's light and grace among men. Scripture does not suggest that the sin of the world is passed on to each person by generation, that is, by the procreative acts that lead to his coming into being. It seems to suggest, rather, that it is passed on by society, culture, upbringing, and the experience of human relationships.

This notion is obvious when you consider problems like racial discrimination. What is transmitted by birth is only the belonging to one or another race. Birth, however, inevitably involves the person who is born in the racial prejudice that is in the world, either as a victim or as one involved in the group that is the oppressor. Man cannot live as though racial discrimination had never happened. He has to live with the ugly consequences and try to find his way out of the situation in which he was born. In a sense he inherited it by generation, and yet it has nothing to do with the act of generation itself.

On the other hand, Dubarle also considered a possibility that perhaps original sin could be interpreted as simply the incomplete state of human evolution, or the natural wastage that goes with any evolutionary process. From his study of Scripture, however, he concluded that the doctrine means more than that. It certainly means that there is a disorder in the world which is the result of sin and which affects everyone. So much is everyone involved in it that even when a child is born, his start in life is already to some extent spoiled and made difficult because of the general state of sin.

This point about the newborn child is, as Father Schoonenberg points out, a crucial one. Actually, our theology of original sin developed out of questions about infant baptism in the third century. Infant baptism seems to have bothered the Eastern and Western Church alike at that time, for Origen, Tertullian, and Cyprian were all writing about it. It had become customary to baptize babies, but baptism had always been explained as being for the remission of sins. People were asking, of course, what sins the babies had committed, and they were told that there were "real stains of sin" in everybody, incurred through birth into the human family.

Later, the Pelagians held that it was all just a question of bad example. When something has been done once, or many times, the unimaginable crime becomes quite imaginable, and it is easier for others to do the same. In response to this statement, Augustine insisted that more than bad example was at stake, and that the key culprit was one person, Adam. Augustine saw Adam as incorporating within himself all his posterity and as poisoning them at the root of their existence when he sinned. St. Thomas, in his time, endorsed the idea that the sin was passed on by generation.

Yet the theologians were never very satisfied with the explanations which seemed to imply that unbaptized infants who died would be damned. Because no one really wanted to say that, theologians continued to look for ways to get around it, knowing that none of us could have much respect for a God who would torture babies.

The official statements of the Councils of the Church did little to help us with the interpretation, because they were all formulated within the symbolism of Adam as the one original ancestor who once possessed something that he lost and could not pass on. Moreover, the statements of the Council of Trent and of subsequent Popes were directed against particular opponents with problems different from ours. Against Luther, for instance, they maintained that baptism really remits original sin, and does not just cover it up.

Putting together all the theological developments and the official statements of the Church, Schoonenberg draws some conclusions about what is essential to the doctrine. He points out how often the Councils reiterated that they only wanted to endorse the teaching of St. Paul in his letter to the Romans. In other words, when our understanding of the interpretation of Scripture advances, the conciliar teaching has to be interpreted accordingly. The teaching of Trent emphasizes that original sin is a moral and religious problem, and it is more helpful to concentrate on that idea rather than on trying to imagine what powers and gifts men might have if it were not for original sin.

More important is the insistence that original sin means present involvement in sinful situations, but that there is a difference between it and the guiltiness of personal sins. Original sin makes it more difficult to live a properly integrated life, not only because of something in the material universe but because of a disorientation in man himself, which applies to everyone born into the human race and belonging to the family of Adam.

Schoonenberg points out that the question of whether original sin is a stain on the individual soul or an involvement in the universal sinful situation, is probably not a good one. Obviously, the first statement is a metaphor, because a stain is something material and souls cannot be stained. The issue is whether the inner reality of the person's life and being is affected or not.

Today we are more aware that a person does not come into the world at birth fully constituted. He is born inarticulate and undetermined, with all kinds of possibilities for development in various directions. Yet he is not free to choose all the directions, because it takes quite a long time before he can begin to take control of his own life and actions. Before he arrives at any point of self-determination, many choices have been made for him, and he has been shaped, conditioned, and directed by others. It is true to say, therefore, that the situation is a part of the person himself, perhaps even a larger part than heredity.

Whereas in the past, the reality of original sin was more vivid to people when explained in terms of physical heredity, today it is more vivid when explained in terms of the whole situation in which man is born. What is important is to make sure we realize the need of redemption by God's grace for everyone.

Father Schoonenberg suggests that if we interpret the classic doctrine of original sin properly, in terms meaningful for our time and also true to tradition, we may find it is very close to (and, perhaps, identical with) the biblical teaching of the sin of the world. The interpretations of Catholic theology today seem to be moving in that direction, and many Catholics are finding it very helpful to think in these terms in order to live a fully Christian life in modern society.

EIGHT

What Morality Did Jesus Teach?

RUDOLF SCHNACKENBURG, BERNARD HAERING

The last chapter discussed the changing focus in our understanding of original sin. A similar development has been going on in our understanding of the idea of personal sin, and therefore, in our whole understanding of morality. Many new situations have arisen in our world. We have had to ask how to decide what is the right thing to do in matters that never arose before, such as the morality of organ transplants, new ways of prolonging life and of controlling the frequency of births, as well as many questions to do with morality in the public life of nations.

In a society where life does not change too much, it is enough to have a code or list of commandments for people to obey. The people need not always know why something must be done or not done. If they obey the code of rules, they can be sure they are living in harmony with God's will and that they will also have harmony in their society. Of course, the code must be right in the first place.

Christian theology compiled its code in the past, and the code became very elaborate and detailed for Catholics. In the last few centuries we had moral theology manuals that ran into several thick volumes; they worked out all sorts of cases that might possibly arise in different circumstances. They were intended first and foremost as handbooks for confessors, that is, as helps in judging actions that had already been done. The manuals also influenced preaching, however, and the content of catechetical teaching. Preaching and teaching, however, are different from judgments in the confessional because they influence the ideals and goals that people set for themselves.

In the compiling of such manuals the moral theologians always turned to two sources for their norms of right and wrong. One source was the teaching of the Church as it already existed in Scripture and Tradition. The other was common sense or right reason, which came to be formulated in terms of natural law. The reason theologians appealed to common sense, or natural law, was that they were convinced that morality is not arbitrary. God does not invent rules at his whim. The right thing to do is always what is in harmony with the whole plan of creation. As Christians we believe that life is not absurd, but that eventually everything makes sense. Because we are endowed with reason and practical common sense, we share in the creative wisdom of God and can figure out what is the right thing to do.

What we call the natural law is accessible to everyone because it is a matter of reason. Yet it became clear quite early in the discussion of natural law that intelligent and highly educated people, whose reasoning powers should be very well developed, did not always agree on the right answers in moral issues. Even if scholars and thinkers studied issues and discussed them together, different schools of opinion tended to form. Catholic theology gave the explanation that men's intellects are clouded by original sin, by their involvement in the situation of sin in the world. It is not always possible, therefore, to guarantee that even the most intelligent person will arrive at an unbiased judgment of right and wrong, uninfluenced by personal considerations of convenience, sympathy, and interest.

This is a matter of common observation and experience, and is another aspect of our need of redemption by God's grace. The important question is what we should do to be open to that grace and to learn to make more consistent and true judgments of right and wrong. There arc two ways in which this question has been answered, and the first seems to be the correct one. The first answer suggests that the constant effort of the whole community is involved. There must be an atmosphere of mutual respect and trust in which we try to reach deeper understanding of truth and are willing to receive it from anyone who may have something enlightening to say, whether or not he is an important person, and whether or not he agrees with our own position.

The second answer that has been suggested seems to be self-defeating. It has been said that since men's intellects are clouded by sin, God must have instituted a guaranteed channel of right judgments and information that is not clouded by sin. The one channel that Catholics could appeal to was the *magisterium* of the Church, that is, the teaching authority of the whole Church. Actually, those who invoked this solution confined the teaching authority more or less to the Pope, though it is not clear why they confined it that way. In other words, if the Pope declared something to be natural law, it was guaranteed to be right reason even though many other people inside and outside the Church might be demonstrating quite convincingly that it was not logical.

This solution is self-defeating because it actually combines the two sources of morality into one. Only authority is left, for human reason and common sense have been eliminated. This is unfortunate because the point of the natural law theory in the Catholic Church was precisely to guarantee a place for reason and to show the continuity between reason and revelation. It is also bad because it makes people passive in their moral responsibilities. It leaves only one obligation, to obey explicit commands. We know that this sort of obedience-morality leads to situ-

ations like that of Nazi Germany, in which a man feels
justified in murdering large numbers of men, women, and
children if his proper superior commands it. The solution
is bad for a third reason. It evokes that "hot line to
heaven" theory which was discussed in Chapter III and
found to be false and out of tune with Catholic tradition.

Actually, there is still one other dimension of natural
law to consider. Common sense judgments do not come out
of the blue, as if all their ancestors were abstract ideas.
Common sense judgments are formed in particular situations, from actual experience. This difference in situations
can account for some very important differences in judgments of what is right according to natural law. It can
account, for instance, for the difference in judgment between Pope Paul VI and the majority of the people on his
commission to study the issue of birth control. It can account for the difference between the earlier official teaching
of the Church forbidding all interest on loans, and its
present cheerful endorsement of installment purchasing,
banking, educational loans with interest, mortgages on
housing, and similar transactions. It can account for many
instances in which the official teaching of the Church was
changed completely in moral matters. They were common
sense or natural law judgments of what was right, based
on the situations that arose. When the situations changed,
the teaching had to change.

If, however, there are two sources for Christian moral
teaching, and not everything is decided by right reason,
an important question arises. It is important to know
whether all the teachings of morality are in the control of
the Church and can be changed by the Church, or whether
some questions have been divinely settled and laid down
at the beginning by Jesus so that they can never be
changed. This question is being asked, for instance, about
divorce. It is important to try to find out what exactly was
characteristic of the moral teaching of Jesus, what made

it different from natural law, and what were the elements He Himself considered basic and essential.

It is a question the tradition has asked for a long time, and the answers have been fairly consistent. We have the gospel accounts of the answer that Jesus gave. Everything is summed up in the command to love God wholeheartedly, and to love each human person as oneself because he is just like oneself and our destinies are intimately intertwined. Whenever theologians have seriously reflected on the matter, they have given the same answer: basically, Christian morality consists of the love of God and the recognition of every man as one's brother whose destiny is bound up with one's own.

Yet theologians have had some hesitation about leaving the matter there. Obviously, if they say no more than that, they leave open the question of what the love of God and the love of neighbor really means. A man still must have some way of finding out what he should do in the actual circumstances of his life.

St. Augustine was asked by the catechists of his diocese what they should tell adult converts about the behavior expected of them as Christians. He thought about it, told them they should instruct their converts in the ten commandments, and then added that actually there are only the two commandments of the love of God and the love of neighbor. What is very interesting to notice is that he evidently did not think he could just give them the last piece of advice without the instruction of the ten commandments first.

This is more or less the pattern that has been followed in catechetics and preaching ever since. It has led people to ask the obvious question whether there is any difference between Jewish and Christian morality, that is, whether Jesus took over the moral teaching of his Hebrew tradition or whether, in some way, he changed it or added to it. It has sometimes been said by Christians that the Jews follow a religion of fear and the Christians one of love, that the Jews are concerned with the letter of the law and the Christians with the spirit of the law. Nothing could be more false; there is no difference of this kind between the two traditions of morality. Both aim at a life motivated by love, and both aim at discerning the wisdom of God which is the spirit of every good law. Both have some ritual laws, designed to give a sense of community and make it possible for people to worship together. Both have some regulations that govern any organized activities.

Some people have felt quite threatened or worried to find out what a good way of life Judaism is, as if its goodness somehow cast doubts on their faith in their own Christian tradition. It is almost as though they felt Christianity could not be right unless Judaism were shown to be very bad and corrupt. Actually, Christianity cannot be right in the morality it teaches unless Judaism is also right in its own morality, for the former is totally grounded in the latter.

Two theologians of our time who have particularly concerned themselves with determining what is essential and what is new in the teachings of Jesus are Rudolf Schnackenburg and Bernard Haering. Rudolf Schnackenburg is a biblical scholar who has written several very important books, among them *The Moral Teaching of the New Testament*. In this book he shows that Jesus did not teach a moral theology at all. For himself he accepted the Jewish law according to the spirit of that law. He obeyed everything, including ritual laws, unless it was in conflict with some urgent demand the Father was making on him in terms of his personal vocation. He often protested in favor of the true traditional understanding of the law against those who made it perfunctory and external. This is the kind of protest that is constantly needed in the Christian community because in Christianity people will be found who make the observances perfunctory and external.

Schnackenburg describes the attitude of Jesus to the
law as a radical one. He tried to offer people the insight
and motivation that would make living according to God's
will absolutely simple, removing any kind of anxiety about
a multiplicity of rules one might transgress. This simplicity is important today for Catholics, and it is why the
Eucharistic fast and the laws of fast and abstinence have
been relaxed and simplified. To be worried about complicated regulations rather than about wholehearted service
of God is as far from the spirit of Jesus as it is off-center
in the tradition of Judaism. Jesus is radical in another
way. He used the style of prophetic proclamation, so that
his moral demands are expressed in extreme and absolute
terms. To interpret his language properly, one must also
look at the gospel accounts of how he acted in relation to
individual people. He shows an extraordinary compassion
to many people who fall far short of the demands he
makes in his preaching.

The basic moral demands of Jesus are repentance, faith,
and discipleship. What is most important is the total personal option for God's will, so that God's will may unfold
before the believer step by step for the rest of his life. The
believer stands before the invitation of God, which may take
all manner of unexpected turns. The most important conclusion that Schnackenburg draws from his detailed study
of the morality of the New Testament is that there is *no*
New Testament code of morality. The Christian ethic, by
its very nature, is open to the future, to new demands in
new situations.

Bernard Haering, at present the outstanding moral theologian of the Catholic Church, has reflected for a long time
on the implications of the openness to the future and the
new demands. Among the many books he has written is a
complete moral theology entitled *The Law of Christ*, but a
short book that brings his most important ideas up-to-date
is *This Time of Salvation*.

Father Haering sees Christian morality as centering on

the concept of *kairos*, the time of faith, of salvation, of opportunity. We need codes of behavior as support or guidelines, but walking within the code, the important point is to be alert to the invitation of God hidden in the circumstances of the moment. No code can ever predict the possibilities of grace and salvation, the opportunities of loving response open to any person at any time.

Jesus himself followed the biblical notion of *kairos* when he spoke of his hour which had not yet come, or his hour which was coming. It meant the moment of opportunity that the Father was opening out before him. If there is something new and different in the moral teaching of Jesus, the newness and distinctiveness is in himself. In his person he opens up the possibilities of the time of redemption, of the moment of opportunity. In fact, there is only one time when Jesus said he was teaching a new commandment, and this commandment was that we should love one another as he loved us. Because he is there as the second Adam, the beginning of trust around which mankind can be rebuilt, his presence is a new commandment, the command to respond to the time of salvation.

One may look at the matter from a slightly different point of view and say that what is new about the morality taught by Jesus is that we are to imitate him or, in the biblical words, to follow him. The central tenet of that following is to live by the breath of the Spirit, responding confidently to the invitation of God's grace as it arises spontaneously within one's life.

There is one aspect of the matter of morality that raises problems. It is the question of whether the inspiration of God could ever be in conflict with a law of the Church or the standard moral teaching. The whole prophetic tradition within the Bible suggests that there can be a conflict. On the other hand, we know that normally we must obey the laws given us by our tradition in order to be in harmony with God and men. The problem is how one would test the spirit of an inspiration that suggests the breaking of a law.

The only answer to this problem seems to be that for oneself, one has to be hesitant to break laws, but from the living experience of the tradition, one must judge what is most in line with the spirit of the law. For others, it is always well to judge very cautiously and to assume that they are in good faith and that they may have seen more or further into the law of Christ than we have. One who obeys the law grudgingly, by fulfilling only the minimal requirements, is never sufficiently in possession of the tradition to have a real freedom within it. Only someone who lives the tradition with a passion will know it from the inside sufficiently that he can have the freedom of the Spirit and really live by the *kairos* morality preached by Jesus.

NINE

Should Christians Renounce the World or Change it?

HENRI DE LUBAC, JOHANN BAPTIST METZ

Connected with Haering's account of the characteristic Christian *kairos* morality is a topic with which many Catholics feel uncomfortable. It is the question of the Christian's relationships with this world—with government, international affairs, urban planning, political parties, and public responsibility in general. Some Catholics do not like to hear religion and politics mentioned in the same sentence and feel affronted when a priest preaches about race relations, poverty programs, or peace from the pulpit. They feel that the only political subject that should be mentioned from the pulpit is a condemnation of Communism. Otherwise, the preacher should concern himself with religion and let the politicians worry about the world and its affairs.

The theological answer to this is that Christianity, that is, the following of Christ, is concerned not only with religion but with all relationships between human persons and groups, whether on a large or small scale. Christianity is as much concerned with war, peace, poverty, and race relations as it is with the sanctity and permanence of marriage and with questions concerning birth control. In both cases Christianity is concerned with these matters because they are the human relationships that constitute our lives. They are our way of living together in the world and expressing the acceptance of our common destiny—expressing it well or badly, as the case may be.

There is a good reason, however, why many Catholics want to lead a good life without reference to the public affairs of society. This reason is partly theological and partly historical. In the time of the apostles the young Christian community, including the writers of the earlier New Testament documents, believed that history had more or less come to an end with Christ, and that the second coming and consummation of the world would happen almost immediately. This was no time to worry about politics or economics. The Lord would come soon and he who believed would be saved. It was the business of the Christian, of every Christian, to preach about the world that was to come, not to concern himself with this world that had already passed away. The early Christians had an immense sense of urgency about the Lord's coming.

There was an even stronger reason for the young Christian community to stay away from public affairs. They knew Jesus had resisted all attempts to sweep him into the Zealot movement which wanted to establish God's kingdom by fighting a war to liberate Israel from the pagan Roman domination. In fact, Jesus had said that his kingdom was not of this world, meaning that he could not establish God's reign in men's hearts by the use of any kind of force. The young Christian community was under pressure for some time, as Jesus had been, to join the Zealots. They knew it was not the Lord's way and that they had to refuse.

For the next several centuries, there was no danger of Christian involvement in the public affairs of the Empire because the Christians were so constantly persecuted that

they had little power to influence either public policy or
affairs of state. From subjects of persecution they became
members of the establishment in the Eastern Roman empire and later in the Christian West. There developed a
tendency to believe that the Empire *was* the kingdom of
God; and the Europe of a later period was referred to as
Christendom. The role of the Christian was to obey Christian princes uncritically, and problems arose only where
there were clashes of political interest between Popes or
bishops and other princes.

In modern times, the governments of the Western world
have tended to be Protestant, secular, or anti-clerical. In
this situation, Popes and bishops have had little in history
to turn to for guidance. They have tended to warn their
people to stay away from politics and involvement in affairs of State because the Popes considered these governments evil. There arose a tendency to invoke the thinking
of the earliest days, and to insist that Christians should
concern themselves not with this world but with the world
to come.

The logic of this thinking, however, was much more difficult to follow in the modern context in which people expected the world to go on for some time yet. It raised
awkward problems because those who do not participate in
public affairs have only themselves to blame if the policies
of the nation are conducted in a godless way. Moreover,
the situation became very complicated when Catholics re-
fused to participate in politics *per se*, but called for separate Catholic schools supported by tax funds and the
exemption of Church property from taxation. Some of the
anomalies of this situation have driven contemporary theologians to reexamine the whole question of the Christian's
relationship to the world as a whole.

Many contemporary theologians have been concerned
with this area, and most of them were stimulated by the
thoughts and writings of Teilhard de Chardin which echo

continuously in the long Vatican II document *Gaudium et Spes,* or *The Church in the Modern World.* In this document there is much discussion of man's vocation in the world in terms of his participation in the work of creation, by transforming the material world to serve the interests of mankind and by transforming human relationships and communications in favor of peace and brotherhood. This discussion, however, always points to a more ultimate goal, a more ultimate destiny which is outside the scope of history. The document further discusses man's principal obligations in the developing society and economy of the world.

One of the theologians who has lectured and written about the *Constitution on the Church in the Modern World* is Henri de Lubac, whose discussion of nature and grace was considered in Chapter VI. Recognizing the thoughts of his friend Teilhard de Chardin in much of the formulation, Father de Lubac, who was himself one of the official experts at the Council (like many of the theologians cited in this book), is convinced that the Council document did not solve all the problems it claims to have solved. The document calls for Christian participation in the development of technology, and in the constructing of a better human society throughout the world. It says that the world must be brought to its fulfillment before it can be transformed.

As de Lubac points out, the document raises and leaves unsolved some very important questions about the value of human work in the world. Does our technological progress help to bring about the kingdom of God in the world, or is it simply providing us with more or less irrelevant "busy-work" to keep us occupied until the end of the world? Are we building in the world the real kingdom to come, or just doing our homework because it is good for us, though it will all be destroyed and a new heaven and a new earth will be created by God without our assistance?

When technological progress is expressed this way, the notion of our building, generation after generation, knowledge and material things that will simply be swept away, is repugnant. Under these circumstances, no one could have much motivation to better conditions in the world for others after his death, for everyone's final happiness would be provided by God whether we work for it or not. Yet there is a deep underlying assumption in much of Christian preaching and literature that the world we live in is ultimately valueless, that human progress counts for nothing, and that only religious duties are worthwhile in the end.

What is basically at stake is our eschatology, that is, our teaching about the Last Things. What the Bible tells us, and tradition has handed down, is in symbolic form and language and needs much interpretation. In this field of eschatology we have done very little of the work of interpretation yet. In fact, we have tended to handle the symbolic statements as though they were already philosophical interpretations. The result has been a general discouragement of Christians from working hard to solve problems in this world—a trend which Marxists noticed from the beginning and constantly criticized and condemned.

A theologian who has begun to work on this problem systematically is a former student of Karl Rahner, Johann Baptist Metz. He starts out from Rahner's position on eschatology: Rahner has pointed out that we do not know the future the same way we know the past, as if a scene were passing before our eyes. We do not know the "how" of the future and, in the case of the absolute future, we cannot even begin to imagine this "how." All that we really know is the demand that the future makes on us in the present, that is to say, what we have to do to go to meet it or to shape it.

J. B. Metz has carried Rahner's ideas further. He believes that when a man is oriented to the future that he does not yet know but which is gradually unfolding for him, his attitude to the world is not so much contemplative as practical. He learns not by looking but by doing because he is not waiting for the next world to come but feels committed to build a new world. Therefore, says Metz in his book *Theology of the World*, the theologians must begin to work on an interpretation of eschatology that shows the relationship to the secular progress of the world.

First of all, the world in terms of biblical thought is not just a place but history itself—history that is always moving toward the fulfillment of God's promises. The powers of this world, which are spoken of as evil, are the forces that hold history back from its fulfillment. The proper relationship between the Christian and the world is what Metz calls a creative and militant eschatology. This means that the Christian must be constantly trying to make the world of men meet the promises of God. He must do this by using all his creative imagination and by finding out in action what the possibilities are.

The traditional teaching of renunciation of the world is not eliminated in this interpretation. One must constantly renounce the comfortable *status quo* in working toward a better future for everyone. It is not action in the world that is to be renounced, but one's own exclusive and reactionary stake in the present development—the privileged status of being white where black people do the menial work and enjoy less of everything including fresh air, the promotion of the economic development of one's own country by crushing smaller countries out of competition, the exclusion of the poor from sight in the modern city. These are examples of the evil world that must pass away so that we can move forward toward the fulfillment of God's promises.

In this view of the world as history and Christian life as creative eschatology, it is no longer possible to contrast

the Church and the world. They are not mutually exclusive. Christians are as much in and of the world as everyone else is. But the Church is supposed to be the community of the promise, the community that makes God's
promise already present in this stage of history. When we
celebrate the sacraments, our celebration is a pledge and a
witness of the promises of God—God's pledge and witness
which we express, and our pledge and witness to the task
we are involved in bringing to fulfillment. But the Church
is not involved in the task simply by praying about it and
watching to see what will happen. The Church, which in
this instance means all Christians, must be involved in
making it happen.

Today's Christians, however, cannot expect to work according to a blueprint. They are called on to be creative
with the possibilities they discover in the world, and to
learn the possibilities in the action. It is in this sense, and
in this sense only, that there must be a separation of
Church and State. The office-holders of the Church cannot hand out a program to Christians telling them exactly what to do in the society in which they live. The
Bible does not provide such a blueprint. The Christian
tradition does not provide it either. We learn more about
the demands of the future on our present when we respond
to what we already know and create solutions to present
problems.

History is full of examples. The first Christians took
slavery for granted as an inevitable feature of human society. The Christian community did, however, insist that
the slaveowner must respect his slaves as brothers in the
Lord, as men having full human dignity. After many centuries Christians began to realize that they should abol-
ish slavery itself because slavery as such was opposed to
the dignity of man. Up to the present time, man has assumed that because poverty is inevitable, the rich should
be charitable to the poor. After many centuries of trying

to practice that charity, we are finally realizing that what we have sometimes called charity was more crushing and humiliating than poverty itself, and that we can eliminate poverty by making jobs and providing guaranteed incomes for all.

In the same way, man once assumed that wars were inevitable, and that not only killing but deliberate torture was an inevitable part of war itself. Then man recognized that there had to be limits to the hurt and injury that could be inflicted on others and, as men tried to observe these limits, they began to see further improvements that were really possible after all. In our century, with the formation of the League of Nations and the United Nations, we have begun to glimpse the possibility of eliminating wars altogether through the use of arbitration techniques. We glimpsed this possibility clearly enough that Pope Paul VI could say with great conviction that there must be no more war, war never again, because it was no longer inevitable. Now that we have glimpsed the possibility we have an obligation to work for it with all the creative imagination we can bring to play in the matter.

If you return, in the light of J. B. Metz's theology of the world and his theology of the last things, to the original question, you will find the answer emerging quite clearly. The Christian does not have the choice whether to renounce the world or to change it. To work creatively to change or transform it is precisely what is meant by renouncing the world.

TEN

Is There Salvation in the Other Religions?

PAUL DEMANN, JEAN DANIELOU, KARL RAHNER

The last chapter and its conclusion raise in a particularly acute form another question the Christian has to ask himself: how does he evaluate the other religions? He finds himself collaborating in the work of transforming the world with people who seem to be striving for the same goals as he is and contributing just as much as he does to their realization. Yet many of these people belong to another religion or faith community.

The question that arises is whether these people participate in the work and the fruits of salvation in spite of their own religious commitment or because of it. Through the ages Christians have given different answers to this question, but the answers have been heavily influenced by their cultural experiences and their national affiliations. It is quite difficult to disentangle the Christian tradition from social and cultural theories held at any particular time. Several Catholic theologians, however, have worked on this question historically.

Before considering Catholic views on the non-Christian religions in general, it must be said that the Christian understanding of Judaism must be discussed separately. The relationship between Judaism and Christianity is unique. The scholar who has done the most work in this field is Paul Démann, who wrote in French, mainly in scattered articles, concerning the relationship of Judaism and Christianity. He made some very important suggestions, but many questions remain unsolved, and a full theology of the Christian understanding of Israel has yet to be published.

It can be said quite clearly that there is salvation in Judaism and that the coming of Jesus in history did not take this salvation away. According to our Scriptures, God made an everlasting covenant with Israel, that they should be his people and that through them all the nations of the earth would be blessed. To generation after generation, God kept promising a new covenant. What it meant was not that the old one would be done away with and another put in its stead, but rather that the old one would become new again as each generation made it its own. It would be written on hearts and not only on tablets of stone left by men's ancestors.

All of these promises have been verified again and again in Judaism. Although Christians have not always been aware of it, Jews have continued through the ages to live with passionate fidelity to the covenant. Under conditions of exile and dispersion, generation after generation has made its own commitment, making the covenant fresh and new in each generation's time.

When the first generation of Christians claimed a new covenant, they were aware of the way the word ''new'' had always been intended in the prophetic writings. Later Christians were to use the terms New and Old Covenant, with the assumption that the Old had become outdated. This is a mistaken interpretation, and even the facts of history contradict it. The Jews have been faithful to the covenant in large numbers, even to the point of martyrdom, and Scripture tells us that God does not desert those who are faithful to him.

Some people think the issue is very simple. If the Jews had really been faithful to the covenant they would have recognized Jesus of Nazareth as Messiah, and thus they would have been included in the new covenant. But since they did not recognize Jesus as Messiah, we can assume that they were not faithful to the covenant. For this reason, history left them behind and they are considered to be lost.

This view leaves all kinds of questions out of account. Even if it was perfectly clear that Jesus was the Messiah, one has to consider the Jews of the dispersion to whom the gospel was never preached. Then one has to ask when it was that their covenant went out of date—whether it was at Pentecost, or at the death of the last apostle, or at some other point. In addition, you also have to ask whether the Jewish participation in the covenant will not go out of date until the end of time.

The only contact that many Jews through the centuries had with Christians and the Christian gospel was that of persecution and victimization in the name of that gospel. In addition, many Jews were told to renounce their religion in favor of Christianity. If someone persecuted you on account of your Christian religion and told you to recant your faith, you would not see this action as the call of God. You would rather think that to be faithful to God you would have to face even martyrdom.

We must face the possibility that Jews cannot accept that Jesus is the expected Messiah because he is not yet Messiah. We who are the presence of Jesus in the world have not yet brought about the signs of the Messianic times. We know what those signs are because the prophetic literature is full of them and the gospels tell us how Jesus quoted them.

The signs of the Messianic times are peace among nations and peoples, perfect brotherhood among men, justice for the poor and the defenseless, no more violence and hatred, and all men coming together to worship one God in their own ways in peace and without persecution. When Paul wrote about these signs, he said by way of illustration that in Christ there cannot be discrimination between Jews and Gentiles, between the cultured Greeks and the poor primitive barbarians, between men who had all kinds of civic rights and women who did not. Today, by way of illustration, we would have to say that in Christ there can be no discrimination between white and black, no advantage taken by rich nations at the expense of poor nations, no wars that destroy small and defenseless countries.

If there is to be no distinction between Jew and gentile in Christ, this means more than the emancipation of Christians from the ritual laws of the Jewish people. There can be no prejudice propagated against the Jews in the name of Christianity, no derogatory remarks, mean jokes, or untrue generalizations. Christians cannot talk or think as if they were a master race or super people. Most of all, there cannot be persecution of the Jews either on account of religion or on account of blood.

If we see any of these injustices, we know that the signs of the Messianic times are not being realized, and the gospel of Jesus is not really being preached. The Nazi holocaust, and the silence of the Christian nations in face of it, proclaimed to the Jews of our century as loud as the blare of trumpets that the Messianic times are not yet. And because the Jewish community continues to be faithful, our own Scriptures tell us that God is faithful to them.

Because the case of Judaism is absolutely unique, theologians have had to ask throughout the ages how Christians are to consider the other religions. From the beginning it was always considered apostasy for Christians to participate in the worship of pagan gods or to offer incense before idols, even the statue of the Emperor. In those days no distinction was made between the use of incense in a ceremony that actually symbolized civil obedience and the pledge of loyalty to the head of state, and the use of incense in what would be, strictly speaking, worship. On account of that lack of distinction, many Christians died. Today, anthropologists would probably help us out of the dilemma by distinguishing between what is actually religious ritual and what is only a very solemn form of civic ritual. In modern times this distinction was made in China and Japan so that Christians could participate in civil ceremonies and the honoring of their ancestors.

The case of the incense-burning before the Emperor's statue, however, shows how strongly the early Christians felt about even the semblance of idolatry. It is all the more striking, then, that they did not always think these things were so terrible when they were done by pagans, but only when they were done by those who had been enlightened by Christ. St. Justin the Martyr, for instance, saw all the pagan philosophies and religions as ways that were leading people forward and would eventually converge on Christ, thereby bringing everyone to the worship of the Father. It is true that he thought the pagans of his time ought to be ready to recognize this and make the final step. In fact, he was quite impatient with them, and felt that a logical and reasonable exposition should convince them that Christianity was the next step.

This understanding seemed to fade in the course of Christian history. Much of it was due to decline in culture in which the universal outlook was lost, and people became much more narrow-minded in secular matters. We know how much this tendency influenced religion, and how complete the general distrust of foreign people and cultures was, from the fact that the Western crusaders even killed Eastern Christians, thinking that they were doing a meritorious work on behalf of Christianity.

Against this kind of background, it is easier to understand how the earlier view of the non-Christian religions as different ways of the different peoples to the same God could have given way to the notion that other ways of worship were inherently evil and could only lead the people who followed them to eternal damnation.

We know that some of the greatest Christian missionary saints sincerely believed that God would commit to the flames of hell all those who were not baptized into the Church, even if they lived in perfectly good faith. They were great saints but they were badly mistaken. We also know that Christian missionaries in Asia frequently forced converts to Christianity to renounce all their previous strivings after God as utterly sinful, made them renounce many social and cultural patterns of their own countries, and made them adopt Western ways that had nothing to do with religion. These missionaries were zealous apostles, but they were wrong. Apparently, it was very difficult in most of Christian history to distinguish between cultural and social customs on the one hand, and religious convictions and ceremonies on the other. Many extremely cruel things were done to converts because of this inability to distinguish between rituals.

In modern times, the development of the social sciences has made it much easier for us to make some of the necessary distinctions between rituals. As missionaries and mission theorists began, step-by-step, to try to understand the cultures and ways of thought of the non-Christian (mainly Asian and African) people, they began also to understand the non-Christian's religious convictions from within, as the people themselves saw them.

Earlier Christians had been so shy of being involved in idolatry and false worship that they really only noticed the unimportant and ludicrous features of those religions. Christians looked at them from the outside and saw a caricature, and then condemned the caricature as if it were the whole reality. When Christians began to study the other religions as they looked from the inside, they often saw something very beautiful, just as a person who looks at the windows of a church from the outside and is unimpressed, changes his mind when he sees the same stained glass windows from the inside.

In response to this problem, one French Jesuit biblical and patristic scholar, Jean Daniélou, who has had close links with missionaries, wrote a series of books and articles, among them *The Salvation of the Nations*. He proposed that we should think of the position of the great Eastern religions as being pre-Christian but leading to Christ. In other words, their followers can be saved by virtue of their religious commitment, that is, by virtue of the hope that implicitly looks to a future fulfillment. The fact that historically in our time these people live *after* the time of Christ is not important because, in experience, they are *before* Christ as long as they have not heard the gospel in a form which makes sense to them.

This holds true not only for the whole nation, people, or faith community, but also for individuals. While there is one Hindu living the Hindu tradition in good faith and with conviction, we cannot speak of the Hindu religion as a false religion.

Because he has given much thought and attention to the study of religious symbolism, in his later writings Daniélou goes even further. He suggests that it is not only because of their sincerity, and their striving after God as best they know how, that God must surely come to meet the Hindus and other non-Christian faith communities. It is also because their striving and their beliefs are true.

We now realize that all our religious language, in Christianity as elsewhere, is symbolic in a special way. It describes realities which we have barely glimpsed, and can never comprehend, by comparison or analogy with things that we know from everyday existence. In the Jewish tradition, it was an important principle not to make images of

God, because all images are false, and the only image of God is man himself. So we speak of God guardedly, as though God were a human person. We give him the masculine gender, make him a father, have him think, speak, get angry, and change his mind. These characteristics are not literally true about God, but they are true in another sense. They are true of our experience of God, and help us to understand the relationship we have with God.

In Hindu and other traditions, the rules of sacred language are different. But these faith communities also know that language cannot be literally true about God. They express their experience of God in those images and analogies that best help them to understand their relationship with God and to focus their response to God. In general, it may be said that the tendency of Asian people is more contemplative than that of the Western world. Many Asians like to leave symbols in their symbolic form, rather than embark on logical explanations of them. Where the Hebrews avoided concrete images of God, the Hindus, if they can, avoid philosophical explanations of God. The Hindus say that when you have images, you understand that you are making only a remote comparison, but when you have explanations, you might be misled into thinking you understand much more than you do. God cannot be understood.

When Christians begin to realize the nature of symbolism, as it is used in religious thought and religious practice, they become much more cautious about speaking of false gods and false religions. Moreover, the more the Christian understands the symbolism, the more he comes to realize how constantly all religions tend more and more to the worship of one God.

This realization does raise the question whether all nations are saved through Jesus Christ, or whether Jesus is not, as we have been taught, the universal savior. This is a question that Karl Rahner has studied over a period of

many years. His conclusion is very simple: in the sense
that only those are saved who acknowledge him explicitly
and by name, Jesus is not the universal savior. Yet Christians are committed by their faith to an understanding of
history that sees Jesus as the focus of it for everyone.

Rahner sees these two statements as quite compatible.
He says that without acclaiming Jesus by name, many
people are, in fact, his followers because they are doing
the will of the Father and working toward the reconciliation of God and men and of men among themselves.
Rahner can show in the gospels many sayings of Jesus that
point in this direction. There is his comment to the disciples that it is not those who acknowledge him and hail
him as Lord that will enter the kingdom of heaven, but
rather those who do the will of the Father. And there is
the famous sketch of the last judgment in Matthew 25,
in which those who have cared for the hungry, the sick,
and the imprisoned are called into the kingdom, and those
who have not done these things are excluded, whether or
not they recognize Jesus as Savior.

To take the words of Jesus seriously, and to apply them
to the circumstances of the twentieth century, leads to
some startling conclusions. Not only the Hindus and the
Buddhists, but also the ''lapsed Catholics'' and the Com-
munists, may enter the kingdom of God to the exclusion of
churchgoers, if the former are living in the world so as
to bring about the Messianic times, and if the latter are
not living their lives in the world in the way that they
should.

Salvation is not an arbitrary reward for hitting upon
the right words in creedal formulations. It is the inner
fruit of a life of love and welcome to God and to all mankind.

What Should You Read Next?

If you have finished reading this book, you may have additional questions that have not been answered. You also may wish to follow up the information contained in the individual topics at more length. Some chapters suggest a wider selection of additional readings than do others.

The subject matter in Chapter I has not yet been written up in a single volume that would be easy to read. Two books that are not directly on the topic may, however, be very helpful: Karl Rahner's *The Christian of the Future*, and Yves Congar's *A History of Theology*.

By far the best and most readable books on the subject matter contained in Chapter II are Gabriel Moran's *The Theology of Revelation* and *The Catechesis of Revelation*.

The subject matter of Chapter III is probably most clearly and concisely developed in the last section of Hans Küng's *The Church*.

In relation to Chapter IV, no doubt the best book to read for a complete survey of how eucharistic doctrine developed is Joseph M. Powers' *Eucharistic Theology*. You may then be interested enough to want to read also Edward Schillebeeckx's *The Eucharist*.

On the subject matter of Chapters V and VII, you will

find a brief, readable, and good presentation in Peter de Rosa's *Christ and Original Sin.*

On the subject of Chapter VI, it is quite difficult to make any recommendations. The best brief account is the separately published essay by Karl Rahner, *Nature and Grace,* but even this is quite technical in its vocabulary. Brilliant insights into the experience of grace can be found in Rosemary Haughton's *Why Be a Christian?*

The best book to read on the question of Chapter VIII is an extremely brief one by Gerard Sloyan, *How Do I Know I'm Doing Right?*, one of the Christian Experience series published by Pflaum Press. There are several other books in that series you might enjoy reading, but if you want to read something longer, you might try Bernard Haering's *This Time of Salvation,* or Rudolf Schnackenburg's, *The Morality of the New Testament.*

On the topics of Chapters IX and X, the best thing to read is Avery Dulles' *The Dimensions of the Church.* You may also want to read *Faith and Freedom* by Barbara Ward.

The publishers and dates of the books recommended here have not been given because most are available in several editions. It is always well to check the current list of paperbacks in print unless you particularly want to buy a hardback book.

These recommendations include only Catholic authors. There is much that Catholics can learn from the Protestant theologians of our time, but that is the subject of another book.